TOWARD STANDARDS

NATURE IN AMERICAN LITERATURE
AMERICAN CRITICISM
THE AMERICAN SCHOLAR
HUMANISM AND AMERICA (EDITOR)

TOWARD STANDARDS

A STUDY OF
THE PRESENT CRITICAL MOVEMENT
IN AMERICAN LETTERS

BY

NORMAN FOERSTER

Director of the School of Letters
University of Iowa

FARRAR & RINEHART
INCORPORATED
ON MURRAY HILL   NEW YORK

PS
78
.F6

TO WILLA CATHER
AND ROBERT FROST

CONTENTS

CONTENTS

6 May 36

PREFACE

As HARRY HANSEN, a competent observer of literary affairs, has recently remarked, the central fact in American literature at the beginning of the 1930's is "the complete bankruptcy of the naturalistic movement." Its proud assurance is gone. It has finally made revolt conventional and uninteresting. It is breaking up in disillusionment and futilitarianism. It is on the defensive, betraying its disorder in a continuous series of petty counterattacks against the advancing force of a movement toward human standards.

The need of standards in life, in art, in criticism is more and more apparent, and naturalism has failed to provide standards. Naturalism has prided itself upon its humble devotion to science, presumed to be the only respectable authority in modern thought, forgetting that, whatever science may do for us, it cannot give us standards. Science gives us natural knowledge, not human objectives. Often, besides, it gives us natural guesses rather than knowl-

edge, in which case it is merely pseudo-science—
an extraordinarily popular "authority" in modern
thought.

But the general public has begun to sense the
limits and dangers of the scientific view of life and
to suspect the seemingly austere "truth" of naturalistic literature. Without strenuously exerting itself,
it is looking for standards wherever they are promised: standards that might discipline the modern
temper, standards suggesting whither mankind
should aim, standards underlying the preface and
eventually the book of morals, standards rendering
mankind human and not merely natural. This ex-
plains why the humanism of Babbitt and More
became, at the turn of the decade, a topic of not
too serious discussion at the dinner table and in the
pullman car. Advertised in this fashion, it has
roused every manner of attack on the part of the
bright young modernists of the press, and at the
same time has impressed the thinking public, neces-
sarily always small in number, as a vital force in
the intellectual situation confronting the twentieth
century. In a century that seems unlikely to achieve
a great religious revival, the fundamental conflict
may well turn out to be one between a modern naturalism seeking further developments and applica-

tions of scientific technique, and a new humanism based upon the whole of human experience.

Even in the universities humanism is becoming a subject of discussion. Though its leaders have been university professors (more or less isolated from the public, like the scientists), the universities have hitherto offered stout resistance, even in the field of letters, to anything not in the usual sense scientific or pseudo-scientific. A change of attitude is now in progress. One indication is the growing interest in literary criticism: new courses are being offered and textbooks are being written, generally by professors so intent upon being discreetly neutral that they can scarcely be said even to have a point of view. It should be possible, however, to have a point of view and at the same time to deal fairly with those who have other points of view.

Now in criticism there are, broadly speaking, three possible points of view. Readers of Matthew Arnold will remember his clear-minded statement, novel in its day, of the three "estimates" used by critics of literature: the personal estimate, the historical estimate, and the real estimate. Literature may count to us personally, may be measured by our personal likings, affinities, and circumstances. Or it may count to us historically, may be measured in terms of its importance, representativeness, and influence viewed in relation to its time and place. Or it may count to us really, may be measured by its approximation to what is really great in literature and valuable to mankind through the ages.

It happens that today all of these estimates are prominent. The personal estimate is that of the impressionists, concerned with the sensations they experience in contact with literary works. The historical estimate is that of the historians of literature, whether they are researchers in the past, reporters of the present, or prophets of the future: in any case they view literary works in relation to the "vital forces" of the time, and, except when unfaithful to their principles, are at bottom deterministic naturalists. The real estimate is that of their chief opponents, the humanists, who seek to transcend not only the personal but also the historical estimate and to attain a judgment in terms of permanently human values. Whereas the criterion of the impressionists is relative to the individual creator or critic, and that of the historians is relative to the age and nation, the criterion of the humanists is relative to nothing less than mankind.

The object of this book is to outline the claims set forth by these three groups of critics and thus

to throw some light upon the conflict in which they
are engaged. I have tried to find the fundamental
issues. I have tried to invite deliberation rather
than prejudice. I have tried to assist the reader to
take a stand based on conviction.

My first effort in this sort was made in the concluding chapter of AMERICAN CRITICISM, written in
the winter of 1926–27 and published in the spring
of 1928. Since that book in the main purported to
be a work of historical-critical exegesis in the field
of scholarship, the journalist reviewers naturally
enough ignored the bulk of it and concentrated upon
my discussion, in the last chapter, of the contemporary struggle between humanism and naturism.
This chapter is now reprinted, with the generous
permission of the publishers, the Houghton Mifflin
Company, in a setting of more general interest.
In other chapters of the present book I have expanded my discussion of naturism by analyzing the
point of view of the impressionists, both the romantic and the skeptical groups, and the point of
view of the historians, both the journalist and the
prophetic groups. I have also expanded my discussion of humanism by relating our present academic humanists with the Humanists of the Renaissance, in a paper read in February, 1930, at a joint

PREFACE

meeting of the Erasmus Club of Duke University
and the Philological Club of the University of North
Carolina. Finally, I have presented my view of the
relation of humanism and religion in a note published in *The Forum* and in *The Criterion*. Three
of the chapters first appeared in *The Bookman*.
Originally, however, most of the chapters were
written with this book in prospect.

N. F.

August, 1930

[xiv]

HUMANISM IN THE
RENAISSANCE

Any open-eyed observer can see that an era of American literary criticism is well under way.

Henry S. Canby, 1922

The critical movement is undoubtedly the most significant movement in our literature during the last decade or so.

Van Wyck Brooks, 1928

A few writers [humanist critics] . . . are doing altogether the most original and aggressive work we can show to the world,—a work more noteworthy, I make bold to say, than anything of its kind now done in England and equal to anything produced in France.

Paul Elmer More, 1928

CHAPTER ONE

HUMANISM IN THE RENAISSANCE

History provides the light of experience—a cumulative wisdom.—Vergerius

Érasme est l'homme de la Renaissance. S'il faut choisir un nom pour caractériser cette période glorieuse, le sien vient le premier à l'esprit.—Pierre de Nolhac

A T A TIME when the word humanist is applied to a pragmatist like Schiller of Oxford, to a modern stoic like Walter Lippmann, to literary scientists like Professors Kittredge and Carleton Brown, to scholarly moralists like Professors Babbitt and More, to Roman Catholics like Monsieur Maritain and adventurous Protestants like Dr. Potter, to anti-Christian socialists like Leon Samson, and even to field naturalists like William Beebe; at a time when, in short, everybody is said to be a humanist, perhaps something might be done to clear up our confusion by turning back to Erasmus, one of the patterns of humanism by universal consent,

[3]

and to the great movement in which he was a pro-
tagonist and in which the stage of modern life and
thought was set.

Whatever humanism may be today, we assume
that it stands for something definite when applied
to the Renaissance. But it does not. Despite our
complacent assurance that our scholarship is scientific, the use of the word in the historical studies
that everyone consults is not really clear and consistent. Sometimes a distinction is made between
a narrower and a broader sense of the term, with
ambiguous results in practice. Sometimes in place
of a broader sense the word paganism is employed,
but this word again is used ambiguously, with reference either to antique life as a whole or to its un-
abashed fleshliness. Sometimes the word humanism
is applied to the all-sided man, the *uomo universale;*
sometimes to the "poet-scholar"; sometimes to men
who were mainly or exclusively poets; sometimes to
painters as well, or to painters who owed a debt to
antiquity, or to painters because of their exuberance
or because of their restraint—though it is also true
that the painters are more generally contrasted with
the humanists. Sometimes science is conceived as
a part of humanism, because the humanists included
the science of the ancients in their literary studies;

[4]

more often it is contrasted with humanism, because
they were not interested in the direct observation
of nature.[1] Sometimes Christianity is conceived as
blended into humanism, because various humanists
found the philosophy of Christianity substantially
the same as that of the ancients; more often it is
contrasted with humanism, because the organized
Church and humanism were indeed two things.[2] One
writer goes so far as to carry on his discussion of
humanism under the heading "The Natural Man,"
frankly reducing what he calls the humanism of

[1] Certainly the humanists showed scant interest in what we
regard as science today. As Burckhardt remarks, "Humanism . . .
attracted to itself the best strength of the nation, and thereby, no
doubt, did injury to the inductive investigation of nature" (THE
CIVILIZATION OF THE ITALIAN RENAISSANCE, 1921, p. 291). George
Sarton speaks bluntly of the Italian Renaissance "contempt of
science," of "the anti-scientific tendencies of the humanists," their
devotion to beauty rather than "truth," their looking "backward
not forward," their acceptance of "the authority of the ancients."
"The only remedy which could have cured them," he concludes,
"was a direct appeal to nature—experimental science—but this was
hardly understood until the following century. It is for that essential reason that the Renaissance was not a scientific renaissance
but a period of dissolution and transition" (J. W. Thompson and
others, THE CIVILIZATION OF THE RENAISSANCE, 1929, pp. 75–95).

[2] If none of the humanists were scientific in our sense, some of
the greater humanists were markedly religious in our sense. Historically, indeed, humanism and religion have almost always been
allies, humanism and science almost never. On the relation of
humanism and religion today, see the note, p. 197.

Erasmus to the usual nineteenth-century blend of "naturalism and humanitarianism"![3]

It is small wonder that humanism today is an elusive concept, when not even our erudite historians can tell us plainly what humanism was in the Renaissance. For the most part, they do not define the word at all; they simply use it, in a sense more or less fluctuating. Yet intelligent discussion demands a firm use based on a definition. Though I have no special competence in the field of the Renaissance, I am going to try to work out a definition both historically sound and permanently suggestive.

In the first place, there is at least dictionary authority for the tendency to distinguish between humanism with a small *h* and Humanism with a capital *H,* a distinction which, if generally agreed upon, would avoid much confusion. (The distinction will be observed in the remainder of this chapter.) Written with a small *h,* the word stands for a general idea, an attitude toward life or way of life. It represents man's effort to define or realize his humanity as distinguished from his animality, on the one hand, and his divinity on the other. Since there may be many ways of conceiving of man's distinctive humanity, we may allow the word to cover all

[3] J. H. Randall, THE MAKING OF THE MODERN MIND, 1926, p. 133.

[6 [

of these ways. It is thus possible to speak of the humanism of persons as various as Aristotle, Confucius, Horace, Erasmus, Goethe, Dr. Johnson, and Irving Babbitt.

In addition to this general meaning, there is also an historical meaning, determined by the great age in which the word Humanist was first used, the Renaissance. The motivating idea of the Renaissance was man's humanity, in opposition to the mediæval idea of man's possible divinity and the modern idea of man's sheer naturalness. To the Renaissance, it was literature that counted centrally, as before it had been religion and afterwards was to be science. A whole age more or less consciously devoted its main energy to realizing, with the aid of classical literature, the idea of humanity, and the word Humanism, when referring to that particular age, may advisedly be written as a proper noun. Thus humanism in lower case refers to a general idea, and Humanism capitalized to a single movement in history. Rightly to define Humanism in this historical sense, then, we must find a definition that will both fit the particular movement and relate the movement to the general idea. Such a definition will define the species within the genus. It will

[7]

attend not only to the temporary and incidental, but also to the permanent and essential. For Renaissance Humanism was only one manifestation of the perennial effort of mankind to understand and express its humanity.

I

To simplify our task, we may separate Italian and Transalpine Humanism. What was Italian Humanism? Or, to use the more concrete and historical term, what was an Italian Humanist?

In the first place, he was a scholar in the field of classical literature. The term *umanista* was applied to a man who devoted himself to *litteræ humaniores* —a student of a body of literature emphasizing man's humanity. Paraphrasing Gellius, the Humanist Battista Guarino wrote in 1459:

> To each species of creatures has been allotted a peculiar and distinctive gift. To horses galloping, to birds flying, comes naturally. To man only is given the desire to learn. Hence what the Greeks called παιδεία we call *studia humanitatis*. For learning and training in Virtue are peculiar to man; therefore our forefathers called them *Humanitas*, the pursuits, the activities, proper to mankind. And no branch of knowledge embraces so wide a range of subjects as that [literary] learning which I have now attempted to describe.

[8]

In similar strain another Humanist, Aeneas Sylvius Piccolomini, wrote to his nephew:

> Without literature, I do not know what you can be, but a two-legged donkey. For, without learning, what is man, however wealthy, however powerful he may be? No one, neither nobleman nor king nor general, is of any worth, if he is ignorant of Letters. . . . Perhaps some maiden fair to see, who is herself attracted by your comeliness, has smitten you, and is entangling you in her coils. You may deem yourself happy in your wooing, but you are being deeply deceived. For, while you are doting on her beauty, you are deserting another beautiful form, that is really fairer by far. For neither the star of morning nor the evening-star is fairer than the wisdom that is won by the study of Letters.

To the Humanists in general, the desire to learn, or rather the desire to learn classical letters, was apparently the clearest proof of man's humanity, his distinctive virtue. The word virtue, indeed, which had meant manliness in the Roman age, and goodness in the Mediæval age, meant in the Revival of Learning chiefly the knowledge of Latin.[4] For two centuries the Humanists regarded Latin as the only language worth writing,[5] the imperial language of learning and letters, and looked with disdain upon

[4] J. E. Sandys, HARVARD LECTURES ON THE REVIVAL OF LEARNING, 1905, p. 56.

[5] J. Burckhardt, *op. cit.*, p. 252.

the unlettered herd to whom "virtue" was impossible. They displayed their attainments all over Italy, declaring that "wherever a learned man fixes his seat, there is home."

Let us remember that they devoted themselves neither to religion, which concerns the plane above the human, nor to natural science, which concerns the plane below. The leading task of the fifteenth and sixteenth centuries was the recovery and imitation of the humanistic literature of the ancients, whose authority in letters was to last till the Romantic Movement of the eighteenth century, as it was to last in the field of education till the latter part of the nineteenth century, when it was gradually superseded by the authority of the modern sciences and modern languages.

Now, the establishment of a neo-classicism capable of enduring for hundreds of years was a task calling not only for extraordinary zeal but also for a courageous confrontation of a series of more particular tasks. The programme of any humanism must be relative to the cultural situation at the time, and must change with the time. Thus the Renaissance, just because it was a movement, not a static condition but a development, constantly altered its emphasis, its interests, its activities in response to its altering needs—a fact not without significance for scholarship in the twentieth century, as I wish to suggest later. It is noteworthy for us that, as the Renaissance progressed, Italian Humanism went through a series of phases, or epochs.

The first epoch has been designated as that of inspiration and discovery. The Revival of Learning naturally began with an enthusiastic appreciation and diffusion of the already known treasure of classical letters. The next step was the search for unknown manuscripts: the exploration of monastic libraries in Italy, France, Switzerland, and Germany. But for the indefatigable collectors of the fourteenth and fifteenth centuries, we should certainly possess only a small portion of the classical literature, especially Greek literature, which we now have. Gradually, as the rewards of this search diminished, the epoch of discovery passed into an epoch of arrangement and translation: the epoch of Cosimo de' Medici at Florence, Alfonso the Magnanimous at Naples, and Nicholas V in Rome; the epoch of the great libraries at Florence, at Urbino, at Rome, at Venice; the epoch of universities, where scholars were trained, and of nobles who competed for their services; the epoch of Humanists like Poggio, Filelfo, and Valla, and, more and more, of pedants miscalled Humanists; the epoch of translators, who made accessible to educated readers virtually the whole *corpus* of Greek classics. Learning had now been revived, but the true culmination of the movement came in the succeeding epoch, an epoch of a more cultivated scholarship, largely associated with academies that sprang up in Florence, Rome, Venice, and throughout Italy, and typified by a man like Poliziano, who was both a distinguished Italian poet and an accomplished Humanist. At home in Greek as well as Latin literature, Poliziano possessed a wide range of knowledge, but he differed more essentially from his predecessors by virtue of a comprehensive conception of scholarship that fused knowledge with taste, insight, and critical sense. While scholarship was thus reaching its high-water mark, the new art of printing was giving fresh impetus to the Revival, and, by rendering learning less esoteric, was bringing about the decay of the prestige of the Humanists themselves. The fourth and last epoch was marked by the ascendency of general culture over Humanist learning. As one historian puts it,

The learning possessed at first by a few teachers, acquired with effort, and communicated with condescension, had now become the common property of cultivated men. It was necessary that the man of letters, educated

HUMANISM IN THE RENAISSANCE

by antiquity, should give proof of his genius by some
originality of mind. The age of acquisition had ended;
the age of application had begun.[6]

Poliziano was succeeded by Bembo, that notorious
"ape of Cicero," and presently the Catholic Reformation forced Italy to resign to northern Europe
the attainments of the age of application.

In the whole of this developing movement, from
Petrarch to Bembo, the typical Humanist was evi-
dently different from the typical scholar of the
present day. The divergence is indicated in part
by Burckhardt's usual synonym for the word Humanist, namely, "poet-scholar" (*Poetphilolog*), or
by Symonds' statement that throughout the periods
of the Revival philology and poetry went hand in
hand. Poliziano, for example, was not only concerned with the chronology of Cicero's FAMILIAR
LETTERS, the details of the discovery of purple dye,
and the differences between the aorist and the imperfect in the signatures of Greek sculptors; he was
equally concerned with the creation of poetry, and
passionately recited his own productions in his lectures at Florence. The ancient classics were not
simply material for erudition; they were also objects of creative imitation and emulation. And they

[6] J. A. Symonds, THE REVIVAL OF LEARNING, 1877, p. 393.

[13]

were objects, also, of literary criticism. Although
criticism did not progress far, prior to the sixteenth
century commentaries on Aristotle's POETICS, the
delight of the Humanists in the ancient literature,
their conviction that it merited imitation and emulation, was itself a salient manifestation of the
critical faculty. To be quite accurate, we must call
the Humanist a scholar-poet-critic.[7]

We have already surpassed the bounds of what
is now conventionally regarded as scholarship, but
still have much farther to go. After all, if it was
necessary for expert learning to open up antiquity,
it was necessary not for the sake of learning nor
for the sake of antiquity but for the sake of life.
The life of the Renaissance had for its aim, as we
have seen, the understanding and realization of
man's humanism as distinguished from his supposed
divinity. New values took the place of the values
cultivated by the Middle Ages. Now, the quest
of values is the quest of criticism, and it is plain that
the Humanists were critics in a sense far deeper
than I have yet intimated. The formal values of
antique literature they elaborately praised and

[7] In A HISTORY OF LITERARY CRITICISM IN THE RENAISSANCE, 1899,
1908, p. vii, J. E. Spingarn concludes that "The birth of modern
criticism was due to the critical activity of Italian humanism."

copied, but at bottom it was the quality of life represented in that literature which fascinated them. Whatever excesses we may observe in their emphasis on form, we are bound to perceive on reflection that what the age passionately desired was a conception of the good life—that old conception of a many-sided, harmonious life of which classic form was the external manifestation. The Italian Humanists were more than men of learning and poets; they were also critics in that wide and profound sense which involves the affirmation of a view of life.

The fundamental motive of Italian Humanism was a reaffirmation of the good life of the ancients. The humanism of Greece and Rome was to be reborn into the world. But among the rank and file of the votaries of pagan antiquity, and even among the leaders themselves, practice lagged so far behind theory that this reborn humanism must be regarded as an illegitimate child. If ancient humanism be defined as a reconciliation of vital energy and ethical control, it is plain that Italian Humanism cultivated the one at the expense of the other.

Since the Renaissance was historically a revolt or emancipation from the real and presumed bondage of the Middle Ages, it naturally drew its inspiration primarily from that expansive energy which permeates Latin and especially Greek culture. The Humanists cultivated the antique flexibility of intelligence and emotion, eager acceptance of the varied powers of human nature; they were enamored of diversity, versatility, many-sidedness, all-sidedness. How far this ideal was consciously drawn from the ancients, and how far it derived from the new modern sense of personality and individualism, it would be venturesome to say; what concerns us here is rather the patent fact that a large part of the old vision of life reappears in the *uomo universale.* The type is already adumbrated by Dante, Petrarch, and Boccaccio, but it belongs especially to the fifteenth century. As one authority points out,

There is no biography which does not, besides the chief work of its hero, speak of other pursuits all passing beyond the limits of dilettantism. The Florentine merchant and statesman was often learned in both the classical languages; the most famous humanists read the ethics and politics of Aristotle to him and his sons; even the daughters of the house were highly educated. The humanist, on his side, was compelled to the most varied attainments, since his philological learning was not limited, as it is now, to the theoretical knowledge of classical antiquity, but had to serve the practical needs of daily life. While studying Pliny, he made collections of natural history; the geography of the ancients was his guide in treating of modern geography, their history was his pattern in writing contemporary chronicles, even when composed in Italian; he not only translated the comedies of Plautus, but acted as manager when they were put on the stage; every effective form of ancient literature down to the dialogues of Lucian he did his best to imitate; and besides all this, he acted as magistrate, secretary, and diplomatist.[8]

A familiar example of the all-sided man is Leon Battista Alberti, an accomplished musician, a painter and sculptor, an architect, a lover of nature and student of science, a defender of Christianity, a classical scholar, a writer in Latin and Italian of treatises on art, on domestic life, and moral, philosophical, and historical works, together with elegies, eclogues, and speeches of many varieties, and finally a man of such physical strength that, with feet together, he could spring over a man's head.

Here, then, was a reincarnation of the pagan zest for life, mixed, no doubt, with a certain naïve pedantry, but none the less real. Here was a new version of the old conception of man as man, endowed with almost limitless potentialities and free to exploit them. Here was a return to the ideal of culture, observed if not formulated in ancient times, with few exceptions unvalued in the Middle Ages, but now given a vitality that lasted at least

[8] Burckhardt, *op. cit.*, pp. 135–136.

till Goethe. It is a large part of ancient humanism, but it is not the whole.

For there is another part in which the Humanists of Italy were conspicuously weak. How could they reconcile vital energy with ethical control, when they were so dimly aware of the value of ethical control? Diversity they attained, but not harmony. Expansion interested them, but not concentration; inclusiveness but not selection; a vocational multiplicity, not an inner unity; the tangential forces of life, not its firm centrality. As the scholarship of the Renaissance tended to degenerate into mere pedantry,— a pseudo-scholarship,—so its humanism (in the wider sense) tended to degenerate into naturism,— a pseudo-humanism. This seems to me not clearly enough recognized today. We perceive adequately only half of the truth. We do full justice to the erudition of the Humanists and to their many-sidedness, both of which are at times approximated by our own greater scholars. But we live in an age of naturism, of science and romantic expansiveness, and our prepossessions keep us from seeing adequately the other half of the truth, namely, that the Humanists of Italy, as well as some scholars who are styled humanists today, were egregiously lacking in that centrality or inner unity, that firm possession of a scale of values, which marked the humanism of ancient Greece. We do not make it plain that Italian Humanism failed to carry out its own programme.

There were exceptions, no doubt, though it is extremely difficult to find them. According to Burckhardt, "several" persons in the Renaissance attained an "harmonious development of their spiritual and material existence," [9] but the two whom he ventures to name, Dante and Tasso, cannot well be numbered among the Humanists. Among the Humanists themselves, we look in vain for an inner unity based upon ethical control, except in the case of a few men who might appropriately be termed Christian Humanists, Vittorino da Feltre, for example, who, as Sandys puts it, was "a Christian no less than a Humanist." As an educator, Vittorino conceived as his end the creation of "the complete citizen," "the harmonious development of mind, body, and character"; [10] but his means of attaining this end were not limited to the humanistic methods of the ancients. In his view, "Christianity and Humanism were the two coördinate factors necessary to the

[9] *Op. cit.*, p. 134.

[10] This and the following quotations are from W. H. Woodward, VITTORINO DA FELTRE AND OTHER HUMANIST EDUCATORS, 1897, pp. 36, 67, 21.

[19]

development of complete manhood." Although he identified the ethics of the two traditions, he impresses us as having derived his intellectual ideals from the classical but his ethical ideals primarily from the Christian tradition. While owing something to the old Roman discipline, "Vittorino was before all else a Christian imbued with the spirit and the doctrine of his faith. . . . It was this which preserved him from exaggerations and moral perversities which disfigured some of his contemporaries and gave an evil name to a certain type of Humanist." He was pious in religious observance, reverent, humble, unselfish, unworldly, sincere, simple, pure— worthy to be spoken of as καλὸς κάγαθὸς, as even Filelfo perceived, but above all a true Christian. He illustrates the fact, which the Roman Catholic historian is justified in insisting upon, that when the Humanism of the Renaissance attained its admirable end, it did so with the help of the tradition of the Church.

Soon after this early Humanist educator, the type was debased, even by such leaders in scholarship as Poggio, Filelfo, and Valla. "By their vanity, their self-importance, their unchaste lives and still more unchaste writings, their insatiable greed for money and reputation, their scurrilous and ridiculous quar-

rels, they went far to belie the claim of classical
literature to be the most humane of studies." [11]
Pagan self-restraint was the exception; pagan exuberance the rule. Scholars gathered round Humanistic princes like the notorious Sigismondo
Malatesta, who, as Sandys remarks, "combined
some of the worst vices of a savage with a romantic
love of learning." "To over-estimate the moral
corruption of Rome at the beginning of the sixteenth
century is almost impossible." [12] "Virtuous women
had no place" there—though it must be admitted
that in the early Renaissance, at least, the women
had preserved their balance better than the men.
At length, as the sixteenth century wore on, while
the doctrine of Humanism still held force, the class
of Humanists fell into such disgrace that "no one
would consent to be reckoned of their number." [13]
It grew abundantly plain that learning and humanism are not the same thing, and that the cult of the
universal man could easily mean the cult of universal
chaos. In practice, Italian Humanism, from the
emancipation of the fourteenth to the degradation
of the sixteenth century, was largely an assertion

[11] A. Tilley, THE DAWN OF THE FRENCH RENAISSANCE, 1918, p. 15.
[12] Symonds, *op. cit.*, p. 406.
[13] Burckhardt, *op. cit.*, p. 272.

of the natural man: was not humanism but naturism.

It remained for northern Europe to attain a more genuine humanism, combining vital energy with ethical control, as in the scholar-poet Milton, who responded to the Renaissance passion for culture and glory while remembering (in his own words) that "There is not that thing in the world of more grave and urgent importance, throughout the whole life of man, than is discipline." Milton gave consummate expression to that reconciliation of the classical and Christian traditions which we have seen in Vittorino, which reappeared in the puerile, fanciful speculations of Pico della Mirandola, and which constituted the central problem of the Transalpine Humanists, including Erasmus, the greatest figure among them and wisest exponent of the blended might of humanism and religion.

II

To us of the twentieth century, Erasmus is a singularly fascinating person—modern-minded, urbane, witty, free of fanaticism, devoid of affectation, and withal elusive. We conceive him as a man with two natures: scholar and theologian on the one hand, sportive mocker on the other, as he appears, respectively, in the portraits of Matsys and Holbein. We are prone to envy those who not only read his works with the ease of contemporaries but also talked with him face to face, men like Colet, who, says Erasmus, "when I praised Aquinas, . . . after a silence looked sharply at me to see whether I spoke in earnest or in irony, and . . . saw that I spoke from my mind." What would we not give for the light shed on his words by the play of expression on that lean, ardent face, by the modulations of a voice perhaps as subtle as the mind that controlled it? What would we not give to hear Erasmus speak from his mind? "At every stage of the study of Erasmus," says Emerton, "one has to ask first what he believed himself to be doing, then what he wished others to believe he was doing, then what others did think he was doing, and finally what the man actually *was* doing." The main cause of this elusiveness, as I hope to show later, is just the fact that he was indeed an eminent humanist, in the wide sense of the word—a personality rich and vibrant, without a trace of the *grob,* finely tempered in mind and character, restlessly seeking that point of equilibrium or Golden Mean that reconciles opposites. It is easy to understand the extremist, the overt and specific reformer, the fanatic who loses himself in a concrete cause, but the humanist is often misunderstood and misrepresented. Had Erasmus been a fanatic of learning, he would have offered no serious problem.

As a man of learning, he may here be dismissed with few words. It is obvious that he was, like the *umanista* of Italy, a scholar in the field of the classical literatures, superior to the Italian type in breadth of knowledge and command of it. After mastering the Latin authors, he looked upon them as "small brooks and turbid pools" in comparison with the Greeks, in whom he found "the purest fountains and rivers flowing with gold." Though he never equalled Budaeus in familiarity with Greek, he controlled an apparatus, as he terms it, competent for a task invaluable in that day, the task of editing and translating those texts upon which Christian theology rested. To this task he addressed his indomitable energies, perceiving that the programme of scholarship was fixed by the needs of the time. In the world of learning into which he was born, "the prime need was for standard editions to fix texts; not good and thorough editions, but something to begin upon, and as soon as possible . . . —to be amended and improved by the labor of later generations. At Rome a beginning was made with the literature of the Romans; from Germany came the first editions of the Schoolmen: the Aldine firm supplied them for the Greeks. Erasmus' life-work was to do this for the New Testament and the Fathers." [14] He collated manuscripts, he used the best critical principles then available, his commentary was as rational as the state of knowledge permitted, his acumen and clarity rendered his whole work illuminating. Erasmus well understood the distinction between the aimless pedant, at whom he sneers, and the purposeful investigator, of whom he says, "He is occupied with the smallest things, but such as the greatest cannot afford to neglect; he deals with minute points, but such as have serious consequences." In an age of editors, he was one of the ablest and most industrious. Aside from his monumental work in the literature of Christianity, he edited a whole throng of Latin and Greek authors. Unlike many other scholars then and now, "he did not make a study of antiquity for its own sake, but used it as an instrument of culture." [15] Like the Italians, he reflected the aristocratic spirit of the Renaissance—a fact commonly deplored by modern admirers of Luther and democracy. Like

[14] P. S. Allen, ERASMUS' SERVICES TO LEARNING, a lecture read in 1925, p. 8.
[15] Pattison and Allen, ENCYCLOPAEDIA BRITANNICA.

them, too, he was nomadic in his mode of life, never living in one place so long as eight years at a time, and proudly calling himself a "citizen of the world." And of course he wrote in Latin, the language of the world, but incomparably better than the Italians.

For he was not only a man of learning, but also the first true man of letters, it has been said, since the fall of the Roman empire. He is the finest type of the "scholar-poet." Striving as always for a sound equilibrium, he succeeded in avoiding the scholastic extreme of cultivating matter at the expense of form and the usual Humanist extreme of cultivating form at the expense of matter. Against the latter extreme he directed his famous dialogue on the Ciceronian purists, caricaturing them as spending seven years in reading Cicero and seven in imitating him, making a dictionary of all the words, all the phrases, and all the rhythms used by Cicero, living in a house where grace radiated from innumerable portraits of Cicero, and dieting devoutly upon ten currants and three coriander seeds coated with sugar. Actually, as Erasmus points out, Cicero was not perfect, and in any case propriety, rightly viewed, requires us to adapt our writing to our own times. In his own writing, certainly, Erasmus was never the mere copyist, but always the sensitive artist, widening the scope of expression by words without classical precedent, subtly modifying the syntax, and showing, almost alone in that age, that a dead language is capable of transmigration. Even in English dress his letters, the commentary of his ADAGES, his COLLOQUIES, his PRAISE OF FOLLY, deservedly "best sellers" in their day, are still fascinating works of literature. More than a scholar and author, Erasmus was also an educator, a maker of inspired textbooks, spending his life largely in teaching the art of writing.

Finally, as a Humanist, this scholar-poet was at the same time a critic: a keen, witty critic whose standards, if resilient, were essentially based upon the classical harmony of vital energy and ethical control. His expansiveness, his many-sidedness, is not, to be sure, that of the Italians. Despite his command of both pagan and Christian lore, his versatility as scholar and writer, his labors upon texts combined with unstinted service in the practical realm of affairs, educational, political, religious, and his own inner diversity in feeling, thought, and will, it must be admitted that his interests and achievements were far more limited than those of some of the "universal men" of Italy. He was not robust physically, though he wrung from his body energies enough for the work of several men. Reaching Florence in the heart of the Renaissance, he had nothing to say of the Duomo or Santa Maria Novella, and in Rome he showed scant interest in the antiquities, not even knowing where the site of the Capitol is. He did not mention painters or their paintings, except in a general way. Unlike Luther, he did not highly esteem the art of music. He was indifferent to metaphysics. Less serious than these limitations, from the point of view of Humanism, was his apparent aversion to the natural scientists, whom Folly represents as indulging in blind conjectures while Nature laughs at them. A modern biographer like Preserved Smith, with his liberal and humanitarian turn of mind, deplores the coldness of Erasmus toward "the world of poverty and toil and ignorance," though social sympathy is not a part of the Humanism of the Renaissance. Having sharply marked limits in his interests, when compared with a man like Alberti before or Goethe after him, Erasmus would scarcely seem to rank high as a humanist; and yet he does, by general consent. From this fact one can only argue that universality, while a part of the humanist ideal, is subordinate to that other part which makes for control or discipline. The heart of humanism would seem to reside in a certain quality of mind and character, rather than in an assemblage of diverse interests.

At all events, Erasmus was superior, in a certain quality of mind and character, to any other man of his generation. The whole of his writings and the whole of his career,—above all, as I believe, his attitude toward the Reformation,—betoken a remarkable devotion to common sense, reason, and ethical discipline, those powers of man in which reside his essential humanity. Luther complained of Erasmus, despite his very real piety, that he did not "sufficiently reveal Christ and the grace of God, . . . for human considerations prevail with him much more than divine." But this is precisely his distinction as a humanist. He perceived that there is a middle plane, the human, between the natural and the religious: "The spirit," he says, "makes us *gods;* the flesh makes us *beasts;* the soul make us *men.*" Though here following the early Fathers, he is in effect marking off that distinctively human realm in which he chose chiefly to dwell. His final appeal is always to what he terms in a letter "the philosophy of wisdom," [16] as opposed equally to

[16] This was to him identical with "the philosophy of Christ." As a Christian, Erasmus was deeply indebted, on the moral side, to

tyrannous authority and radical reformation, and
the means that he preferred in furthering the philosophy of wisdom was one associated not with Jesus
but with "Saint Socrates," namely, a dry, insinuating
irony that destroys in order to build. Only a prejudiced or dull-minded reader asserts that Erasmus
was a complete scoffer or skeptic; he was, rather,
an earnest seeker after the truth, a lover of distinc-
tions and reservations and limits, almost the only
man of his time who avoided a certain brutality in
the quest of the truth, almost the only man who
saw all the facets of his subject and represented
them with just discrimination. In him the rational
and the ethical met, and criticized and fertilized
each other. His judgments were those of a whole
man.

the Humanist Colet, and on the intellectual side to the Fathers
(above all, the great scholar Jerome), who were *"eux-mêmes des
humanistes avant la lettre."* *"Sa raison s'incline devant les mys-
tères et avoue Jésus-Christ; mais ce Christ est conçu comme 'une
fontaine de science,' comme 'le père de la philosophie.'"* *"Sobriété,
décence, soumission des désirs à la raison, mépris ou aversion des
choses extérieures qui n'apportent que désenchantement et dégoût:
ce programme est tout philosophique; Erasme l'emprunte aux sages
de l'antiquité."* *"Il voit aussi le lien qui unit cette sagesse antique
à la sagesse chrétienne: de l'une à l'autre, il y a continuité pro-
fonde et nécessaire."* (Pineau, ÉRASME, SA PENSÉE RELIGIEUSE, 1924,
pp. 61, 73, 116, 147.)

[30]

How firmly centered he was appears most clearly
in his judgment of the Reformation, despite his
superficial perplexities and vacillations. "In his
own person," as Preserved Smith puts it, "he went
through exactly the same evolution as did the
Renaissance in the whole of western Europe, that
of being at first the preparer, then the moderate
supporter, and finally the enemy, of the Reformation." Professor Smith, writing from the Protestant
point of view, deplores the last step, as other scholars, writing from the Catholic point of view, deplore
the first two steps; but from still another point of
view, that of humanism, it seems to me that Erasmus
was right at every step. To the priest who asserted
that "Erasmus laid the eggs and Luther hatched the
chickens," the proper retort is that of Erasmus
himself: "I laid a hen's egg; Luther hatched a bird
of quite a different breed." The egg promised a
humanized Christianity; the bird hatched by the
Reformation was, as Erasmus soon perceived, not
a humanist creation. While agreeing with many of
the doctrines of the Reformers, he was affronted by
their methods and spirit. "I have seen the hearers
of your sermons come out like men possessed, with
anger and rage painted on their faces. . . . They
came out like warriors, animated by the oration of

[31]

the general to some mighty attack." "I am a lover
of liberty, I cannot and will not serve a party." He
conceived both parties to be straining in the support
of dogmas,—serving the demon of the absolute in
disregard of the many-sidedness of truth,—often
unimportant dogmas, such as the immaculate conception, which he held withdrew attention from the
essential life of Christianity. In the important
question of the freedom of the will, he took, as
usual, a middle position, attributing (as he says)
"much to grace but something to free will," and,
for practical guidance in life, the stand of common
sense: "If we be in the way of piety, let us hasten
on to better things; if involved in sin, let us find
the remedy of repentance." In all the perplexities
that beset a wise man in the conflict between the
religious parties, Erasmus kept his head and steered
a course between the Lutheran Scylla and the Roman
Charybdis, clear-eyed as to the dangers of both
extremes. He came to see, what both parties failed
to see, that the issue had been falsely drawn, that
the true adversaries were not Lutherans against
Romans but both extremes combined against the
cause of humanism. And if he was himself crushed
between the scholastics and evangelics, impotent to
carry the Renaissance on to its true goal; if he stood

neutral above the conflict instead of making his weight count in the historic collision of his age, he could yet serve an aftertime by his loyalty to a noble ideal, an ideal of reasonableness and measure that will always form an essential part of any Christianity worth having, and will remain vital even if Christianity should ever perish from the earth.[17]

III

Such was Erasmus the humanist. The sequel I must sketch rapidly. By the time of his death, virtually the whole of antique literature, both classical and Christian, had been made accessible. The great age of acquisition was over; the next task of scholarship was the development of a literary criticism capable of sustaining a great creative age, the age of Cervantes, of Shakespeare, of Milton, of Molière and Racine, in whom the literary impulse of the humanistic Renaissance attained its culmination.

Then gradually, in the late seventeenth and in the

[17] *"On peut regretter qu'Érasme et ses amis de Rome n'aient pas dirigé leur temps; peut-être l'histoire n'aurait-elle pas à déplorer 'la banqueroute de la Renaissance.' Mais le monde n'écoute pas les hommes sages, mesurés, prudents, les croyants sans fanatisme et les hardis sans témérité. Le monde, dit Érasme, est gouverné par la Folie."* (Pierre de Nolhac, ÉRASME ET L'ITALIE, 1925, p. 86.)

eighteenth century, the humanistic side of the Renaissance subsided, and its naturistic side advanced. A new phase began, so strikingly new that we may almost speak of another Renaissance, the naturistic Renaissance, composed of two movements, the romantic and the scientific. Although these two movements were dependent on each other, they gained the ascendancy in turn, first romanticism, then science. Romanticism, latent in the individualism and naturism of Petrarch and Rabelais, became, in the eighteenth century, a new vision of life postulating the unity, instead of the former dualism, between man and nature. The old conventions were swept aside, and new ones constructed on the pattern of common humanity and primitive man (the noble savage). Primitivism caused the new dispensation to seek its literary models chiefly in writers called "Gothic," whether mediæval or not, who were admired for their naïveté, spontaneity, and organic genius.

The first epoch in this Renaissance may be designated as one of inspiration and criticism. Although for the most part English in origin, it is best exemplified in the awakening of Germany. Only superficially responsive to earlier Italian and French influence, Germany was in the eighteenth century

fertilized by the romantic culture of England—the
original genius of Shakespeare, the touching sim-
plicity of the ballads in Percy's RELIQUES, the sentimental naturism of Ossian, the romantic heresy of
Edward Young that originality in art is "of a vegetable nature; it rises spontaneously from the vital
root of genius; it grows, it is not made," and that
Nature "brings us into the world all originals."
Fanned by Rousseau, these flaming ideas and examples inspired a succession of critical minds,—from
Lessing, Herder, the young Goethe and Schiller, to
the Schlegel brothers,—who worked out the ideology
of romanticism.

The second epoch may be designated as mainly
one of creative application. The splendid energy
of romanticism, using the new examples and ideas,
came to fruition in the English Romantic Movement, in the *romantische Schule,* in *l'école roman-
tique.* Creation in this epoch overshadowed scholarship and criticism.

The third epoch, covering most of the nineteenth
century, and, thus far, three decades of the twentieth, may be termed an epoch of scientific accumulation. Science now gained the ascendancy over
romanticism; as an American scientist once put it,
"Darwin and Huxley became the Erasmus and

Luther of a new reformation." Taking over the romantic interest in origins, in historical change, in the conception of development, science worked out the idea of organic evolution and placed man in nature, not spiritually, as the romantics had sought to do, but physically. Literary scholarship for the first time became thoroughly scientific, in temper and method if not always in results. The study of language, being especially amenable to the method of science, was solidly established by Bopp and Jakob Grimm and carried to something like perfection by the *Junggrammatiker*. Even the study of *litteræ humaniores*, after all that Renaissance Humanism had done, was set on a new plane by Friedrich August Wolf, who awoke in the schools and universities of Germany "an enthusiasm for ancient literature second only to that of the Revival in the sixteenth century." [18] His conception of an *Alterthumswissenschaft* was in the next generation the inspiration of August Boeckh, the leader of the historical and antiquarian school which has made it possible for us really to enter into the life of the ancients. The "historical sense," of which Valla and Erasmus had caught but a glimpse, and of which Winkelmann

[18] J. E. Sandys, A HISTORY OF CLASSICAL SCHOLARSHIP, 1908, vol. III, p. 53.

[36]

and Herder had possessed themselves with a comparatively meagre apparatus of learning, now at length became a prime essential in the progress of research. Exploiting this means to knowledge under the tutelage of the scientific spirit of the age, scholars proceeded to assemble a colossal paraphernalia of universities, libraries, learned societies, learned journals, purified texts, variorum editions, concordances, bibliography, and the card index—a titanic laboratory from which issued an unending stream of small discoveries, now petering out. Modern literary scholarship, like modern war, is conducted on a grand scale, and the armies of workers, invading one province after another till they have virtually conquered the whole world of literary history, are sighing for other worlds to conquer, if only the world of the insignificant.

In their headlong pursuit of linguistic and historical erudition, modern scholars have paid scant attention to literary criticism. Scientific in their methodology in the realm of fact, they are still romantic in their ideology in the realm of value, still thinking in terms of romantic relativity, universal sympathy or indiscrimination, the creative imagination, the sense of wonder, the exaltation of the vital and primitive, the spontaneity of genius,

[37]

the disparagement of reason and ethical restraint, the religion of nature and humanity; are still capable, therefore, of deifying such writers as Blake and Shelley and Whitman, of ranking the NIEBELUNG-ENLIED with the ILIAD, of esteeming Cynewulf as "one of the six or seven great English poets," and of assuming that BEOWULF is more valuable to the graduate student of English than the whole of the Victorian era or the age of Pericles. But these are scholastic after-notions, bearing only the semblance of life. The fact is that the acids of skepticism have eaten into all our critical principles till they have quite disintegrated. As for the creative movement of the past hundred years, it has been in the main a realistic portrayal of actual experience, inspired by the scientific movement and unsupported by scholarship. The divorce of scholarship from contemporary creation, like the divorce of scholarship from criticism, has no parallel in the German eighteenth century or in Erasmus or in the Italian Renaissance. Realism came into literature and is now passing into disintegration, without disturbing the peace of our scholars.

In sum, our present scholarship has developed out of an age of naturism; it is the child of romanticism and science; it has its assumptions and limits, like everything else in history; it reflects the age, and will change with the age, which is now in transition toward a movement not naturistic.

What will this movement be? And what should be the relation of scholarship to it? If we do indeed prize the historical sense, we shall have to apply it to ourselves and our labors. We cannot rest content in the mere continuation of the naturistic scholarship of the nineteenth century. No longer will it suffice to declare, with the complacency of Sidney Lee in his presidential address before the Modern Language Research Association (1918), that the object of literary scholarship is "the addition of new stores to the stock of already available knowledge," in fulfillment of "the wisdom of the greatest of English prophets and champions of research, Francis Bacon," —a thinker who (we are reminded) laid down, as three laws of success in learning, coöperation, scientific method, and enticing money rewards. Happily, there is at least a beginning of doubt in the more recent presidential address of William Albert Nitze before the Modern Language Association of America (1929), an address entitled "Horizons," in which the speaker asserts that the Association has reached a "wakeful state," proposes annual discussion of the "objectives of our scholarship," points out that "unlike science, scholarship deals with 'human' facts, not with external phenomena," and draws inspiration from Emerson rather than Bacon. It is worth noting, however, that Bacon, like other prophets, may be read two ways. Living in an age in many respects similar to ours, he made it plain that knowledge should be gathered not for "its own sake" but for the sake of man. He saw clearly the difference between the mediæval learning of the universities, aloof from the center of vitality in the developing Renaissance, and the new spirit of inquiry into the "secret motions of things" for human ends. He attempted, as we must attempt today, a redefinition of learning and of the relation of learning to the higher objects of human life. The time has come for us, surely, to pass beyond the accumulation of ascertainable facts to the use of facts in the study of values. The time has come for us to lay the foundations of a new humanistic scholarship.

Science cannot help us in this task, for science, while it offers a method in the getting of knowledge, offers no guidance in the using of knowledge. To be sure, all that we do hereafter must be done in the spirit of science—this conviction is the great contribution of the three hundred years since Lord

Bacon. It is equally evident that the quest of new facts should continue, even though it is now yielding returns that are diminishing and disproportionate to the effort. But the central need of scholarship today is the service of a new and higher objective. For this it would be vain to go to the scientist; we must go elsewhere—and where with better promise than to the Humanist of the Renaissance?

I do not mean that we must imitate what was incidental and temporary in the Humanist of that age: his use of Latin, his frenzied erudition, his want of thoroughness and of the historical sense, his nomadic life and loose morals. I mean of course that we may advisedly imitate him in his essential aspects. For the true descendant of the Renaissance Humanist I take to be, first, a sound scholar, secondly, a trained writer if not "poet," and thirdly, a critic of literature and of the subject of literature, life: bold to maintain that man is neither a mere animal, nor a soul in exile, but above all a being "infinite in faculty" and "noble in reason"—a creature impelled, as Erasmus saw, by every manner of Folly, yet capable of self-control through the philosophy of wisdom.

CHAPTER TWO

IMPRESSIONISM

The truth is what appears to each man at each time.
— *Protagoras*

THE VOGUE of impressionistic criticism in America in the twentieth century has been largely the result of revolt against the somewhat obtuse literary scholarship of the colleges and universities. Particularly after the year 1910, large numbers of young men keenly interested in life and in letters refused to follow the lead of the pedants, historians, and scientists of literature who seemed to have the *belles lettres* in their keeping, who proclaimed that literature must be studied laboriously but were never very clear as to why it should be studied at all, who maintained the old traditions as to what authors were important without infusing new vitality into those traditions, who were immensely erudite in their concern for the historical study of literature but appeared to conceive that history came to an end in the nineteenth century if not in the age of

Elizabeth, who wrote books and articles and read papers before the Modern Language Association in a factual and mechanical language that gave scant promise of really illuminating the language of the poets and dramatists, who in their addiction to dates, texts, emendations, influences, evidence external and internal, appeared to have lost the power of enjoying life or literature in terms of feeling, imagination, and reason in its freer activities.

Even if these men of learning had a right to exist (which was more than some of the young rebels conceded), a few of them would surely go a long way, and the huge and ever-growing bulk of such men were betraying the cause that they professed, transforming *litteræ humaniores* into *litteræ inhumaniores*. Against the august scholars who had possessed themselves of the institutions of education a band of bright-minded young intellectuals ranged themselves with more and more confidence; taking the offensive, they remade old organs of opinion and established new ones, and won the ear of the public through their smartness, their alert open-mindedness, their outspokenness, and their advocacy of authors and tendencies whose day was drawing near. At length they carried their impressionistic

[43]

programme to triumph in the years just following the World War.

That impressionism did triumph in these years anyone could readily see, I think, by comparing the American criticism of the nineteenth century, which mainly followed the romantic lawgivers, with a typical post-war book such as the Modern Library anthology entitled A MODERN BOOK OF CRITICISM (1919), edited by Ludwig Lewisohn. In his introduction Mr. Lewisohn finds that the college teacher "devotes himself to formal studies in literary history," while the ordinary journalist expresses "the average tribal reaction to new books and plays," and that the pretensions of the "older group" of critics, such as Paul Elmer More and Irving Babbitt, were demolished years before by a still older group of critics, such as Anatole France and Jules Lemaître, who appear to be the model our emancipated young critics properly imitate. In his lively moral enthusiasm Mr. Lewisohn pictures the allied historical scholars and tribal reviewers as "an army of Goliaths," against whom are arrayed a band of intellectuals "like a troupe of shivering young Davids— slim and frail but with a glint of morning sunshine on their foreheads." I think this is an unduly modest estimate of these young Davids, who, as the his-

IMPRESSIONISM

torical scholar will one day prove to us, at that time
already had victory in their grasp. In the higher
circles of opinion, if not in the provincial newspapers, the impressionists were well established by
1919. Only two years after, when *The New
Republic* invited "a number of contemporary critics"
(deceased and unborn critics having been ruled out),
"representing every school, to give their answer"
to the question "What is the function of criticism?"
it happened that five or six of the seven contributors
came out more or less vigorously for impressionism
—a sufficient indication of the success of the cause.[1]
If these critics indeed represented "every school,"
the schools then existing differed only in their shades
of impressionism, which I take *not* to have been the
fact. For the historian of literature will presently
show us, I suspect, that, though impressionism was
perhaps at its apogee about 1921, other significant
schools not represented in the symposium were then
conceiving otherwise of the function of criticism,
and he will further tell us, I suspect, that, though
impressionism became more general in the ensuing

[1] The contributors to this symposium were Robert Morss Lovett,
H. L. Mencken, J. Middleton Murry, Morris R. Cohen, Dickinson
S. Miller, Clive Bell, and Francis Hackett. *The New Republic,*
Literary Supplement, October 26, 1921.

years, it weakened gradually as its Davids lost full conviction, as leaders of other camps grew in power, and as certain parts of the reading public began to look elsewhere for leaders more likely to cope with the disintegration of modern thought.

The historian will also convince us, we may assert with assurance, that the rise and triumph of impressionism cannot be explained simply as a reaction against academic excesses of philology and historicity. Impressionism is fundamentally a child of the romantic movement of the early nineteenth century. Romanticism, reacting against the pedantry of rules and defects, concerned itself with "beauties" rather than defects and with organic necessity instead of mechanical rules. The best critic, as the practice of Coleridge, Lamb, and Hazlitt seemed to demonstrate in England, is he who is keenly sensitive to impressions, responsive to excellence in many kinds, gifted in intuitive perceptions, contagious in his enthusiasms, rich in personality and in powers of self-expression. These qualities and others appeared later in Sainte-Beuve, one of Arnold's masters, who united in himself the best of the impressionistic and historical lines of development. Arnold himself, though his central tendency was toward humanism, sometimes compromised his humanistic principles

by leaving them vague, so that they could be twisted
to serve the ends of pure impressionism, as in the
case of such catch-words as "disinterestedness,"
"flexibility," and "elasticity." Drawing upon Arnold,
drawing more largely upon a new wave of romantic
feeling that rose in his time, Walter Pater stated
clearly, in the preface and conclusion to STUDIES IN
THE RENAISSANCE, the essential creed of impressionism. Oscar Wilde followed, and Arthur Symons,
and others; in England, as in France, impressionism
triumphed in the *décadence* of the nineteenth century. Its most authoritative pronouncement was in
LA VIE LITTÉRAIRE of Anatole France so long ago
as 1888. Here in America, we have had no Anatole
France; we have had only a Mr. Mencken.

I

Though the creed of the followers of Pater and
Anatole France at first glance appears very simple,
on a near examination it turns out to be singularly
elusive. In theoretical statement, it is one thing;
in practical application, another. Repudiating any
fraternity in taste, and asserting complete liberty
and equality in taste, impressionism in actual practice is much given to making its judgments prevail.
If one chooses to disregard this discrepancy between

[47]

theory and practice on the ground that integrity is not to be looked for in human affairs, one is still confronted with another and more serious discrepancy within the theory itself. Maintaining that impressions are unique and relative to the individual, this theory oscillates between the idea that they are relative to the individual author and the idea that they are relative to the individual critic. There are really two types of impressionistic criticism, one concerned with the uniqueness of the author and the other concerned with the uniqueness of the critic, and between these types most of the work of this school hovers disconcertingly.

One encounters this ambiguity already in Walter Pater, author of the most famous statement of impressionism in English. The first type of impressionism dominates his preface, in which he fundamentally rests his argument on the dictum of Matthew Arnold that the aim of criticism is "to see the object as in itself it really is." If criticism begins when one realizes distinctly one's pleasurable sensations in the presence of an object of art, it attains its end when one defines the special power or force in the object that produced these sensations, when one at length perceives the causative "virtue" that characterizes the work—when the critic "has dis-

[48]

engaged that virtue, and noted it, as a chemist notes some natural element, for himself and others." This is curiously like one of the scientific occupations of the literary historian, who, by eliminating all influences upon a given work, aims to reveal what is unique in that work. In the spirit of the historian Pater goes on to say that the impressionist "will remember always that beauty exists in many forms. To him all periods, types, schools of taste, are in themselves equal." The impressionist differs from the historian, however, in seeking to make his way to all periods, types, and schools of taste, not by means of knowledge of externals but by means of "a certain kind of temperament, the power of being deeply moved by the presence of beautiful objects." In the words of Sainte-Beuve, whom Pater quotes, the rule of the impressionists is *de se borner à connaître de près les belles choses, et à s'en nourrir en exquis amateurs, en humanistes accomplis.*" Through æsthetic appreciation, they seek to know beautiful things intimately, to assimilate the unique virtue of each, and to help others to assimilate this virtue. They believe that the function of the critic is, in plain language, that of an appreciator and a showman.

Now, as I have already suggested, this is only a late form of the romantic theory of criticism, rather than a new theory requiring a new name. According to the romantic theory, the fundamental critical virtue is that of sympathy, the essence of taste is the same as that of creative genius, and the best critic is he who reveals the nature of beautiful things by complete understanding of the creative intent in them. In romantic criticism, beauty has many mansions; strictly, indeed, each author's work, and each work of each author, is an unique organism. Essentially relativistic, romanticism sought to supplant an artificial notion of the unity of man with an organic conception of the uniqueness of men. "I am made unlike anyone I have ever seen"—Rousseau's notorious temperamental declaration of independence— was repeated in substance by a long procession of egos eager to confess and exhibit themselves in all their varied naturalness. Even Emerson, like Eve in Paradise, was fascinated by that mysterious and "peculiar fruit which each man was created to bear." Turning away from the classical and pseudo-classical preoccupation with the normal, the representative, the universal, romanticism gave itself up to a quest of the unusual, the strange, the novel, finding everything admirable so long as it was spontaneous. If it was prejudiced against the age before, for which it had terms of opprobrium like our "Victorian" and

"Puritan," it had on the whole quite as much breadth of sympathy and readiness of gusto as those more recent *exquis amateurs* whom we style impressionists. The appreciator-showman we might more properly style the romanticist, and reserve the new term for the second kind of impressionist, the impressionist impressed with himself.

When the romantic movement had lost its exuberant spirits and high seriousness, it became increasingly doubtful to later critics, romantic in temperament, whether they could really return to the author's vision and perceive the uniqueness of that vision. How, they asked, can we know, as critics, the artistic object as it really is, when we cannot even safely assert, as philosophers, that we know anything? The most that we know is that each of us receives impressions from without, an ever-changing flux of impressions. For us, there is no abiding reality in external nature, the realm of appearance, nor is there any abiding reality in the inner experience of the mind, which is but the scene of personal and fugitive impressions. We cannot escape out of ourselves. If we would be honest, we must rest content with an old Greek formula: "The truth is what *appears* to *each* man at *each* time." This recrudescence of radical impressionism, latent in romantic relativity and abetted by that "keenest skepticism" which, as Huxley asserted, science demanded, is to be found, two years after the lay sermon "On the Advisableness of Improving Natural Knowledge," in the conclusion to Walter Pater's STUDIES IN THE RENAISSANCE. Considered in relation with the preface, this conclusion is violently paradoxical.

Quite in the manner of his twentieth-century descendants, Pater begins with these words: "To regard all things and principles of things as inconstant modes or fashions has more and more become the tendency of modern thought." After proceeding to reduce experience to a swarm of impressions upon the human mind, he reduces it yet further by maintaining that

> Experience . . . is ringed round for each one of us by that thick wall of personality through which no real voice has ever pierced on its way to us, or from us to that which we can only conjecture to be without. Every one of those impressions is the impression of the individual in his isolation, each mind keeping as a solitary prisoner its own dream of a world. Analysis goes a step farther still, and assures us that those impressions of the individual mind to which, for each one of us, experience dwindles down, are in perpetual flight; that each of them is limited by time, and that as time is infinitely divisible, each of them is

infinitely divisible also; all that is actual in it being a
single moment.

Life is, then, made up of these fleeting moments,
and it behoves us to cherish them while we may, to
miss none of them, to feel these pulses of life keenly,
—"to burn always with this hard, gemlike flame,"
instead of forming habits and opinions in a false
and stereotyped existence. This is the ecstasy of
art, above all else; our highest wisdom is "the love
of art for its own sake." "For art," Pater concludes, "comes to you proposing frankly to give
nothing but the highest quality to your moments as
they pass, and simply for those moments' sake."

This indeed is an impressionistic theory of life
and art, and something very different from the
romantic theory to which Pater limited himself in
his preface. There, it will be recalled, one's impression, one's pleasurable sensations in the presence
of an object of art, is only a necessary preliminary,
a means toward the end of criticism, that end being
to see the object as in itself it really it. He does
not doubt, in the preface, that we can so see the
object, that we can *know* beautiful objects intimately,
that we can disengage the virtue that is *in* them,—
not merely in them for us personally,—and that we
can successfully note this virtue for the benefit of

others. With this argument Pater may have reconciled, to his own satisfaction if not to ours, his other
argument that our impressions are forever changing,
that they are merely our personal impressions, and
that the thick wall of personality forbids communication. Such is the experimental disinterestedness,
the flexibility, the elasticity of the impressionist!

When loyal to his creed, the impressionist knows
nothing save that he is the scene of delightful (and
painful) impressions. Although he uses reason to
justify his skepticism, he shares the romanticist's
hostility to reason as a means of perceiving truth.
Although he is a man of feeling, seeking the "unique
pleasure" which each object or moment may bring,
and describing it with a delicate emotional sensitive-
ness, he lacks the romanticist's faith in feeling as a
means of perceiving truth. The pursuit of truth,
indeed, he solemnly or jestingly renounces. He has
only the relative truth of his impressions, and his
life consists in enjoying them and expressing some
of them in a private creative joy (since, strictly, he
cannot communicate them to others). The impressionist, in a word, may be defined as a disillusioned
romantic critic who has turned creator. If he cannot
see artistic objects as they are, if he cannot return
to the impressions which the artists sought to

objectify, if he cannot comprehend the uniqueness of artists, he can yet create new artistic objects by expressing his impression of the objects created by artists, and thus offer his own uniqueness in lieu of that of so-called creative artists. Abandoning as hopeless the task of appreciative criticism, or revelation of the author, he takes refuge in creative criticism, or revelation of the critic. Though what he thinks of a book can have no validity for anyone but himself, the expression of his thought may nevertheless have value as a piece of new creation. It is the book as seen through a temperament, and if the temperament is exceptionally rich and interesting, this expression may also be exceptionally rich and interesting—more so, conceivably, than the book itself. And temperament being, like everything else, in perpetual flux from year to year, month to month, day to day, what is true for it at one time may not be true for it at another. A piece of criticism is thus a fragment of the critic's autobiography; to be exact, it is a given artistic object seen through a given temperament at a given moment.

This creed, so simple in its logic, has been most tellingly advocated by the Gallic mind, above all by Anatole France and Jules Lemaître, whose suave intelligence, urbane irony, and accomplished charm of style have captivated many moderns who might have been less attentive to the same ideas had they been presented through less arresting personalities. How can one answer Lemaître when he writes:

> I assure you, it is possible for me, as for other people, to judge on principles and not on impressions. Only if I did so I should not be sincere. I should say things of which I should not be sure, while I am sure of my impressions. I can, on the whole, only describe myself in my contact with the works that are submitted to me. That can be done without indiscretion or self-conceit, for there is a part of our personality in each of us which can interest everybody. You say this is not criticism? Then it is something else, and I am not greatly concerned about the name you give to what I write.

Is not this candor wholly admirable? Is it possible to answer these simple truths without pedantry, without indiscretion or self-conceit? Who would not prefer the honesty of the master impressionist, Anatole France, to the strained reasoning of the "objective" critic, who, as France reports, accuses him of being

> tainted with subjectivity, the worst of evils; for from subjectivity one sinks into illusion, sensuality, and concupiscence, and one judges human work by the pleasure received therefrom, which is an abomination; because one must not derive pleasure from any intellectual work without knowing whether one is right to be pleased;

because man, being a reasoning animal, must first of all reason; for it is necessary to be right, and not necessary to find gratification; because it is man's business to seek instruction by means of dialectic, which is infallible; because one must always put a truth at the end of a chain of reasoning, like a knot at the end of a thread, since otherwise the reasoning would not hold, and it is necessary that it should, because one attaches thereto several further reasons so as to form an indestructible system which lasts ten years or so.

If we will be honest with ourselves, is not this pretty much what objective criticism comes to? Are we not ready to accept the forthright assertion of Anatole France that

There is no such thing as objective criticism any more than there is objective art, and all who flatter themselves that they put aught but themselves into their work are dupes of the most fallacious illusion. The truth is that one never gets out of oneself (*qu'on ne sort jamais de soi-même*). That is one of our greatest miseries. What would we not give to see, if but for a minute, the sky and the earth with the many-faceted eye of a fly, or to understand nature with the rude and simple brain of an ape? But just that is forbidden us. We cannot, like Tiresias, be men and remember having been women. We are locked into our persons as into a lasting prison.

And is not our effort to emerge from ourselves by our own will uncomfortably like that of the old Nuremberg professor, absorbed in æsthetics, who

[57]

at night used "to exchange his visible body for an astral one, in order to compare the legs of beautiful sleepers with those of the Venus of Praxiteles"? What is there to hinder us, save stubbornness and stupidity, from confessing the plain truth as to what we are doing when we indulge in criticism—when we have not that "strength to be silent" which a faithful skepticism asks of us, asking more than we can give? To be quite frank, the critic ought to say, "Gentlemen, I am going to talk about myself on the subject of Shakespeare, or Racine, or Pascal, or Goethe—subjects that offer me a beautiful opportunity." Are we not ready at last to subscribe to the familiar words: "The good critic is he who relates the adventures of his soul among masterpieces"?

II

Even if we cannot join the impressionists, we must admit that the creed of Anatole France is not only seductive but also, in certain respects, admirable and useful. Apparently taking a hint from Nietzsche, J. E. Spingarn has described the old, old conflict between objective and impressionistic criticism as a conflict between the sexes: "They are," he conceives, "the two sexes of Criticism; and to say that they flourish in every age is to say that every age has its masculine as well as its feminine criticism,—the masculine criticism that may or may not force its own standards on literature, but that never at all events is dominated by the object of its studies; and the feminine criticism that responds to the lure of art with a kind of passive ecstasy." [2]

To deny virtues to feminine (or impressionistic)

---

[2] CREATIVE CRITICISM, 1917, p. 12. Ignoring the eternal triangle involved in this figure—a masculine criticism, a feminine criticism, and an hermaphrodite art—Mr. Spingarn declares that the rival criticisms should be "mystically mated"—presumably in the expressionistic criticism of Croce. The true origin of Croce's theory is, however, to be found in romanticism. As Mr. Spingarn acknowledges, romanticism substituted "expression" for "imitation" as the key to art, and formulated "the principle that art has no aim except expression; that its aim is complete when expression is complete; that 'beauty is its own excuse for being.'" The principle is the source of the æsthetic of Croce, who has indeed "driven home its inevitable consequences" in a set of ideas that many persons have found as alluring as those of radical impressionism. At bottom, they are only a sophisticated form of conservative impressionism, that is, of appreciative or romantic theory. For the identification of genius and taste, e. g., which Mr. Spingarn heralds as "the final achievement of modern thought on the subject of art," one may overlook Croce and go straight back to August Wilhelm Schlegel's lectures in 1803. I cannot see that Croce has done anything more than prolong interest in the cult of appreciation. His work has colored our contemporary speculation far more than our actual practice of criticism, and it has produced no discernible school of critics.

criticism would be, at the least, ungallant. What are these virtues?

1. Foremost is the indispensable virtue of æsthetic responsiveness. Without comprehension of the creative point of view, without intuitive understanding of the author's intention, without openness to the impression that the author strove to convey, the critic cannot hope to see the object as it really is, cannot feel and know it as he must before he can justly criticize it. In the actual practice of criticism, the application of theory to particular works, one must agree with Francis Hackett that the mere "possession of all the best æsthetic theories in the world does not guarantee one syllable of one's criticism," "for without genuine *rapport* there is no spark of life in anything that is written or said about literature." Equally futile is the mere possession of all the best learning in the world, even the historical learning which the scholar fondly values for enabling him to see the real object and to estimate it. Forgetting that historical learning is of small consequence in comparison with intuitive understanding (commonly five or ten percent. of the total means to knowledge, to reduce the matter to scholarly exactness), the modern professor of literature plies a species of scientific research that takes him

farther and farther from literature and renders his casual efforts at criticism sophomoric. The prior condition to all good criticism is a wise passiveness to the will of the author, as even a neo-classicist like Alexander Pope recognized:

> A perfect judge will read each work of wit
> With the same spirit that its author writ.

To this truth Pope and his kind offered little more than lip-service; it remained for later schools of criticism, romantic and impressionistic, to show the full significance of such statements, if also to exaggerate them till their feminine criticism became *voluptueuse*.

2. Vitality of expression, important in all criticism, is a prime virtue of impressionism. Feeling the need of communicating his enjoyment, chaste or voluptuous, the impressionist tends to think of himself, in the phrase of Clive Bell, as "a guide and an animator." Hence he seeks "first to bring his reader into the presence of what he believes to be art, then to cajole or bully him into a receptive frame of mind. He must, therefore, besides conviction, possess a power of persuasion and stimulation." Dullness, deadness, the want of vitality, is never easily pardoned in any writing, creative or critical—

[61]

a fact of which impressionists are, for the most part, well aware. Whether animated by the author's or by their own uniqueness, they want to be and usually are interesting. What life scintillates in the pages of Charles Lamb, what quiet ardor suffuses those of Walter Pater, what subtle perfections of feeling and intelligence lure the reader of Anatole France to the last measured word! These men can write, can animate and stimulate, can speak a living language akin to that of the authors whom we term creative. This mobility of phrase, this instinct for the telling word, this aptness in the revealing image, persuading us insensibly that the writer sees and speaks from within art, is a powerful instrument that every critic should seek to forge for himself.

3. The impressionist is useful in reminding us of the subjective element, the element of uniqueness in men, that forbids a wholly scientific or objective criticism. *L'équation personelle* is a source of distortion even in science, far more in history, and still more in criticism. Without following the radical impressionist into the abyss of pure relativity, the critic must cherish the doubts that send him back to examine his authors and their works afresh, must weigh the force of many opinions at variance with his own, must be quite frank in exposing the funda-

mental assumptions upon which his judgments ultimately rest, and must be content to present his truth
as provisional. His problem, indeed, is the infinitely
delicate one of establishing the mean between the
extremes of dogmatism and pure relativity. Thanks
to the development of relativistic thought that
followed long ages of dogmatic authority, the
twentieth-century critic has this problem more
clearly and squarely before him than it has ever
been before his predecessors.

4. Finally, radical impressionism, by insisting
upon both vitality of expression and the uniqueness
of the critic, has made us fully realize the importance, in criticism, of personality. When Oscar
Wilde says (and Mr. Lovett repeats) that "The
critic occupies the same relation to the work of art
that he criticizes as the artist does to the visible
world of form and color, or the unseen world of
passion and thought," he expresses an idea that an
ancient like Aristotle could not well have grasped
but that nevertheless contains an element of important truth. The ancients did not think of literature,
creative or critical, as self-expression, and if we
moderns think of it as nothing else, we are not
wholly misguided. Although all writers are judged,
in the end, by their truth of vision and mastery of

the art of writing, their truth is still the truth as seen by one man and their mastery is the mastery attained by one man—an agent there must be and his qualities will inevitably color his work. If personality be indeed less valuable than impersonality, it everywhere registers itself in art, in critical as in creative literature, and in this respect creation and criticism are one. We have latterly said much of "creative criticism," meaning either that the critic repeats the creative act or that he becomes a creator in his own right. These seem to me false meanings; but we may properly use the phrase hereafter if we mean by it that criticism reflects personality and therefore belongs less with science than with art.

III

Reacting against the crude dogmas of pseudo-classical criticism in the eighteenth century, and against the factual method of pseudo-scientific scholarship in the nineteenth and twentieth centuries, impressionism has at least aimed at central principles of art and criticism. But it has overshot its mark. I have tried to show how much may be said for it; but more must be said against it.

1. Of "appreciation," the theory of the showman, it suffices to say that it does not constitute criticism.

Despite the etymology and proper meaning of the word, appreciation does not effect an appraisal or evaluation, but accepts the works of art as the scientist accepts the works of nature. Ignoring the fact that art and nature are two things, romantic or appreciative criticism conceives each work of art as an organism developing from within according to a law of its own. It looks for the vital, the spontaneous, the unique, and is content in rendering these plain to those who cannot see them so well as the responsive critic. Ultimately, I fear, the appreciator is merely a teacher of inexperienced readers, an enthusiastic pedagogue, like a certain professor who announced as his theory of teaching literature: "Come on in, boys, the water's fine." To be satisfied with *rapport* and with passing it on to others, is, however, to renounce the immemorial right of criticism to judge art by standards and criteria that transcend the uniqueness of authors and their works. As a matter of fact, every showman, whatever his professions of impartial understanding, has actually decided preferences, and his central task would seem to be not to reject them out of hand, but to examine them earnestly to determine wherein they are personal and wherein they are human. However difficult it may be to determine this distinction, the critic cannot afford to shrink from this task and limit himself to the easier task of accepting every manner of vital uniqueness.

2. The still easier task of independent creation is assuredly not criticism. Aware that he can never attain absolute *rapport,* that he can never hope to see eye to eye with the artist, that, if taste and genius are identical, taste is strictly non-existent, the appreciator more or less candidly turns creator. He is now content to interest himself in the only uniqueness that he deems within his reach, namely, his own, and to regard the products of all other unique individuals as material for his own creative effort, rather than as subjects for objective criticism. If reproached with abandoning the field of criticism, he may reply, as we have seen, that he does not much care what one calls his compositions so long as they are interesting or charming. Surely, however, the question at issue is not a name but that which the name signifies. If the impressionist will give us criticism under another name, we shall be duly grateful; but in truth he does not give it to us at all. He gives us a work of art, which might as well be a lyric or an autobiographic episode as a critical essay. It is, indeed, in a very real sense a lyric or an autobiographic episode—an adventure of the "soul" not

among men or among natural objects but among masterpieces and apprentice-pieces of literature. This is not what we wanted, and I do not see why we should accept something else irrelevant to the purpose in view.

3. If we are told that the wise critic must doubt and finally reject this purpose, we are to assert that skepticism is not the whole of wisdom. While wisdom must entertain doubts, it refuses to serve the one and only and jealous god of doubt. The wisdom we are speaking of is human wisdom, and we must satisfy our humanity, as even Anatole France, most faithful of skeptics, was honest enough to recognize. Pure skepticism, he admitted, would involve us in perfect silence, all speech being affirmation of one sort or other, and from this specter of absolute sterility he confessed that he recoiled. The result was a long series of published affirmations, and one knows not how many hours of oral affirmations. The same paradox is manifest in the works of his vulgarian American miniature, one of our New Republicans, who has habitually regarded other people's truths as prejudices and his own prejudices as truths, even while declaring that truth is "something that is believed in only by persons who have never tried personally to pursue it to its fastnesses and grab it

by the tail." The contemporary impressionist speaks as though the elusiveness of this tail were a new observation in natural history. A rather long time ago, in a firmly ironical passage in one of the Platonic dialogues, Socrates answered the Anatole France of his time, the Sophist Protagoras, who maintained that man is the measure of all things.

> I am charmed with his doctrine [remarks Socrates] that what appears is to each one, but I wonder that he did not begin his book on Truth with a declaration that a pig or a dog-faced baboon, or some other yet stranger monster which has sensation, is the measure of all things; then he might have shown a magnificent contempt for our opinion by informing us at the outset that while we were reverencing him like a God for his wisdom he was no better than a tadpole, not to speak of his fellow-men.[3]

And Socrates continues:

> If truth is only sensation, and no man can discern another's feelings better than he, or has any superior right to determine whether his opinion is true or false, but each . . . is to himself the sole judge, and everything that he judges is true and right, why, my friend, should Protagoras be preferred to the place of wisdom and instruction, and deserve to be well paid, and we poor ignoramuses have to go to him, if each one is the measure of his own wisdom?

[3] Anatole France, it will be recalled, openly coveted the brain of an ape. His is a bolder statement than usual of the modern thirst for the primitive.

It is plain enough that Protagoras, like Anatole France, regarded his own opinions as truer than those of most of his contemporaries, and that not a few of his contemporaries agreed that they were truer, since they paid good coin for them. It is plain enough that the modern impressionists, like other supporters of special theories of life and art, are inly assured that their light is not darkness, and that darkness bedevils those who think otherwise. Analyzed more searchingly than they will analyze themselves, they will be found to agree with Mr. Murry, who, though strongly drawn by the appreciative and creative theories, yet admits that "The critic stands or falls by the stability of his truth," or even with Dr. Johnson, whom Mr. Murry dares to quote in *The New Republic:* "Nothing can please many and please long, but just representations of human nature. . . . The irregular combinations of fanciful invention may delight awhile, by that novelty of which the common satiety of life sends us all in quest; but the pleasures of sudden wonder are soon exhausted, and the mind can repose only on the stability of truth."

4. Impressionism never succeeds in explaining away tradition, that element of permanence which links remote times and places and is hostile to

fundamental alteration. The impressionist argument that tradition is a delusion and does not really exist, cannot be brushed aside as contrary to common sense, since the impressionist does not accept a sense that is common to men. Nor can it be brushed aside as merely sophomoric, an instance of clever foolishness, since the impressionist takes his argument so seriously that it has itself become traditional. This lends it at least the semblance of authority.

More exactly, the argument is that what we term tradition is nothing more than an artificial and spurious consequence of stupid docility. As Anatole France declares, "Some work which, for some reason or other, has, to begin with, gained the suffrages of some, will thereupon gather those of many. The first alone were free; all the others did nothing but obey. They have neither spontaneity, nor insight, nor courage, nor any character. And their multiplication creates fame. It all depends upon a very small beginning." Now, it is plain that tradition does depend upon a very small beginning, but why must we assert that it grows solely by docile imitation, that all those who subscribe to the original opinion are without spontaneity, insight, courage, and any character? Are we to believe that Anatole France himself was without these qualities when he admired masterpieces favored by tradition and thus added his weight to tradition? Is it likely that these qualities are possessed in common by impressionists and by nobody else? Are we to believe that we must look in vain for spontaneity, insight, courage, or character in Lessing, in Dr. Johnson, in Coleridge, in Arnold, all of whom were concerned with tradition, with real estimates as opposed to artificial, with universal judgments as opposed to personal? Is it not men like these who build and maintain, form and reform tradition? They, too, like the leaders of impressionism, have a following largely in consequence of docile imitation; as in all human affairs, there are both leaders and led, and it is the leaders, those superior in the aforesaid qualities, who count most in the establishment and continuance of fame and tradition. Instead of centering his attention upon the leaders, the impressionist chooses to see only the stupidity and hypocrisy of the rank and file, remarking that the works that everybody admires are those which nobody examines (*celles que personne n'examine*). But "nobody" is a large word, which here includes the few but fit somebodies who read and reread the masterpieces. It is significant that even the impressionist speaks of masterpieces, and finds in them some of his most interesting adventures.

When he does turn to the leaders, the impressionist must logically admit that critics like Lessing, Dr. Johnson, Coleridge, and Arnold after all possess independence, since they attain prominence largely by disagreeing with current majority opinions. Furthermore, if they agree as to the masters and masterpieces, they do so for different reasons. If, for example, the fame of Homer, the fame of Shakespeare, continues on its way, its progress is certainly marked with curious contradictions. In the seventeenth century a leader like Boileau praised Homer for having observed the rules of the epic, but today, says Anatole France, we discover and admire in the ILIAD its "barbarous and primitive character." Aside from the fact that this represents adequately neither Boileau nor a modern like Gilbert Murray, it illustrates not only the disagreement of critics but also their independence. Their disagreement as to the reasons for eminence, moreover, arises mainly from the fact that great authors have various sides. We need not think it strange that a critic should emphasize a side neglected by the age before, or serviceable for the needs of his own age; nor must we conclude that he is blind to other sides. That

Gilbert Murray tends to romanticize the Greeks is a natural consequence of his living in an age saturated with romanticism, but it does not mean that his Greeks have nothing in common with those of Jebb or Arnold. That the pseudo-classicists of the eighteenth century tried to fit Shakespeare into the "rules" was inevitable in that age of abstract reason, but it does not mean that they were incapable of responding to Shakespeare on other grounds. For my part, I cannot see anything profound in the assertion of Anatole France that "There is not a single opinion in literature which one cannot easily fight with its precise opposite. Who, then, will be able to end the disputes of the flute-players?" If we will but listen keenly enough, we shall generally find that the flute-players are merely playing different versions of the same tune.

Tradition is indeed a formidable obstacle to those who would make judgment a purely private concern. And theirs is the burden of proof. For tradition is an established fact, as old as human history, capable of endless modification, but impervious to frontal attacks calculated to destroy it, utterly insensitive to the clever paradoxes and shallow logicality of light-armed skeptics. The case against it, indeed, can be proved by one method only: by showing that tradition deceived us in this given instance, then in that instance, and then in every instance. Here is an ambitious task to which impressionists should address themselves at once. If one generation of impressionists can dispose of only a few instances, surely they will have confidence in ultimate victory. And since, as has been said, impressionism also has a tradition, they will have to consider in the end, if not at the beginning, whether their own tradition like all the rest is false.

CHAPTER THREE

HISTORY: JOURNALISM

The notion that literary values are relative to literary periods, that the literature of a period is primarily an expression and a symptom of the time, is so natural to us now that we can hardly detach our minds from it.—
T. S. Eliot

WHEN OUR critics have not been impressionists, they have commonly been historians. While impressionistic criticism, requiring little knowledge or effort of thought, has attracted the rank and file of our slapdash journalists, historical criticism, requiring much knowledge and orderly thought, has attracted some of our more serious journalists and virtually the entire body of scholars in our colleges and universities. Although these historians have often displayed by the way an appreciative or skeptical impressionism, their central task has been the study of literature in relation to the endless permutations of its environment.

For a hundred years, critics and scholars alike

have tended to view literature as a supplement to history. History itself they have conceived as a record of the economic, social, institutional, and political forces of human civilization in their manifold interplay and alteration, and literature as a reflection of these forces. A great writer, it is held, does not write what he wishes to write; he writes what his age gives him to write. If he endeavors to oppose the spirit of his age, he is lost; but if he can unite himself with the central urge of his time, can devote his vital power to expressing the passions governing the society to which he belongs, he will achieve an artistic record of the life of his own age, which is different from the life of all other ages. A new "historical sense" has swept away the old assumption that men in various ages are alike just because they are all men, and it has swept away the corollary to that assumption, that excellence in literature is at all times the same. Instead of speaking of an absolute beauty in literature determined by Homer or Aristotle, we now speak of an absolutely relative beauty determined by the changing interests and ideals of humanity. Increasingly the object of criticism has been, not to judge literature by universal standards, but to understand the pro-

ductions of the different ages. As M. Mornet, for
example, has said,

> Literary history is not separated from general history.
> Since Sainte-Beuve and Taine, our concern is not with
> pursuing sterile dogmatic discussions, but with knowing
> what the work of art is, how it is born and takes its place
> among the forces which incessantly modify the soul and
> human societies (*les forces qui modifient incessament l'âme
> et les sociétés humaines*).

I

It is necessary to glance farther back, however,
than to Sainte-Beuve and Taine. Our preoccupation
with the historical sense, our shift of emphasis from
man himself to the *forces* which incessantly change
him, is a result of the general modern abandonment
of humanism and religion for naturism—that vast
revolution, in the eighteenth and nineteenth centuries, of which the French Revolution may be
termed an external incident. When the ordering of
life and thought by authority was destroyed by
rationalism, the humanistic and Christian traditions,
supported by authority, appeared to be discredited,
and prestige more and more passed to a new outlook
on life, that of naturism: a name embracing both the
romantic movement and the scientific movement.

The inner unity of the romantic and the scientific

movements may be seen, for instance, in the relation of the idea of historical relativity that underlies the romantic movement and the idea of organic evolution that has inspired modern science. As a distinguished American literary scholar has said,

> In the latter half of the eighteenth century there arose an entirely new conception of history and the historical process. It is the discovery of the naive in contrast to the artificial, the sudden realization of the value and importance of the national as opposed to the abstract classical type of humanity, which causes the rise of the new conception of history. . . . Humanity has developed in its diversity and beauty in every clime and under every sky. For the beautiful is no mere abstraction, but variously reveals itself in life. It is the historical point of view from which we comprehend historical variety, through which we perceive and enjoy the beautiful in all its manifestations. . . . It is through Romanticism primarily that the historical method gained its sway.[1]

Rousseau was the first great spokesman of the conviction that the natural is superior to the artificial, that when the individual is natural—obedient to the law of his own genius—he is organically unique and admirable; and Rousseau's German follower, Herder, was the first great spokesman of the idea of cultural relativity, by virtue of which each

[1] Julius Goebel, address of the President, PUBLICATIONS OF THE MODERN LANGUAGE ASSOCIATION, 1915.

age and country that obeys the law of its own genius
is organically unique and admirable. As the new
absorption in the natural man drove romantic
thinkers and dreamers into the primitive past, so the
new absorption in the national genius drove them
into the hitherto despised Middle Age—to its faith,
its art, its vernacular literatures. From this interest
in origins and growth on the part of the romanticists, it is no great step to that interest which later
animated the scientists and which made of evolution
an accepted hypothesis. As Professor Brett has put
it, "The biological movement in the sciences is
equivalent to the romantic movement in literature."[2]

Romanticism and science together prepared the
way for a virtually new kind of literary criticism.
The first great critic who strikes us as thoroughly
modern is Sainte-Beuve, who added to the generous
sympathies of romanticism the industrious exacti-
tude of science. "To be in literary history and in
criticism a disciple of Bacon," as he himself observed, "seemed to me the need of the times." Concerned with understanding and explaining more than
with judging, he studied not only literary works but
their writers, the influences upon them of heredity,
education, and environment; he availed himself of

---

[2] G. S. Brett, PSYCHOLOGY, ANCIENT AND MODERN, 1928, p. 149.

every resource open to the psychologist and historian of souls in order to unlock the heart of his subjects, producing, in the end, a truly remarkable "natural history of intellects and temperaments." Then came Taine, disciple of Sainte-Beuve and Hegel, who created a definite system of the laws to which authors are subject. "You may consider man," he announced, "as an animal of superior species who produces philosophies and poems about as silkworms produce their cocoons and bees their cells." Had not the time arrived to apply the Baconian method, rigorously, to the human species? "Science draws near at last and draws near to man; it has passed the visible and palpable world of stars, plants, and stones to which men had disdainfully confined it; it is laying hold of the soul, having at its disposal all the keen and exact instruments of which three hundred years of experiment have proved the precision and measured the scope." As an exercise in the application of scientific method to the human soul, he wrote his famous HISTORY OF ENGLISH LITERATURE, in which he conceived of the work of art as the joint product of three forces, the Race, the Place, and the Time. It is not for the scientific critic of literature to praise or to blame, any more than it is for the scientific student of nature to praise or to blame. "Criticism," he says, "proceeds like botany, which studies with equal interest at one moment the orange tree, at another the pine; at one moment the laurel, and at another the birch; it is itself a sort of botany applied not to plants but to the works of man." In the flush of the scientific spirit of the age, Taine suffered his zeal to mislead him into premature and rigid generalizations. But at least he made it impossible for any important critic after him to deal with literature *in vacuo*, regardless of its historical relations. It is less true to say that his formula has been rejected, than that it has been endlessly revised and subtilized by his successors, above all, by his highly trained academic successors in Europe and America.

This is not the place for a discussion of academic erudition in the field of literature.[3] After all, the public shows a right instinct in conceiving that criticism and scholarship are, at present, two things, and that accordingly criticism is an activity outside and scholarship an activity inside the university. The typical scholar is well content with his historical learning; austerely factual and objective, at least in

---

[3] I have dealt with this subject in THE AMERICAN SCHOLAR, University of North Carolina Press, 1929, urging a reintegration of scholarship and criticism.

theory, he disparages all criticism as, at bottom, subjective and impressionistic. Obedient to the scientific spirit, he constantly seeks to shut out that personal equation which is prized by the impressionist as the very basis of criticism. And yet the faith that he professes and the faith that he lives by are often at variance, for in practice he does not wholly repress his preferences, nor apparently wish wholly to repress them. These preferences are commonly romantic. As Professor Goebel gratefully acknowledges, "No other great intellectual movement of subsequent years has had so powerful an influence upon the development of our studies as has Romanticism," so that it should surprise no one to find that "scholars are trying to revive the great and fruitful ideas of the Romanticists" [4] and opposing the ideas of the humanists.

II

Although it is generally assumed that a vast abyss separates scholarship and journalism, they are at present aiming at the same object. While alien in method and in spirit, and often mutually exclusive in their subject matter—the one concerning itself

[4] Julius Goebel, *op. cit.*

with the past as if the present did not exist, the other concerning itself with the present as if the past did not exist—scholarship and journalism in twentieth-century America are fundamentally united in their preoccupation with history. There is no great gap between the academic historian who records the literary phenomena of the more remote past and the journalistic historian who reports the literary phenomena of that recent past which we call the present. I am disregarding, of course, the impressionistic journalists, who measure literature by their personal moods; I am speaking of those more serious journalists who endeavor to transcend their personal limitations by considering literature in the light of the forces animating contemporary civilization, especially in their own country. While the scholars explain past literature relatively to the age and land from which it emerged, these journalists explain present literature relatively to the modern world and the national genius. As journalists, they rightly concern themselves with *le jour,* reporting the literary news of the day—the external gossip if they are feeble reporters, the internal goings-on if they are penetrating observers.

The best of our recent or living journalists, significantly, have undergone an elaborate academic

discipline in literary history: men like Carl Van
Doren, Ph.D. (Columbia), Stuart P. Sherman,
Ph.D. (Harvard), and Henry S. Canby, Ph.D.
(Yale). All three, after receiving the stamp of the
doctorate, proceeded to engage in teaching. Perceiving, however, as Dr. Van Doren says, that "the
universities in the United States no longer put such
a shoulder to the wheel of creative literature as
they put there half a century ago," that "the scholars
spend their talents, often admirable, on antiquarian
research, but rarely know or care enough to encour-
age, interpret, or preserve the best that is being
done from year to year," these journalistic historians turned more and more away from the usual
academic study of the best (and much else) that
has been thought and said, to a freer study and
propagation of the best (and much else) that is
being done from year to year and day to day. More
and more unsparingly, they put a shoulder to the
wheel of creative literature.[5]

[5] Dr. Van Doren himself, formerly a member of the Columbia
faculty and headmaster of The Brearley School, as well as man-
aging editor of THE CAMBRIDGE HISTORY OF AMERICAN LITERATURE,
became literary editor of *The Nation* and *The Century Magazine*
and editor of The Literary Guild. In a commentary upon himself
("The Friendly Enemy, Carl Van Doren," MANY MINDS, 1924), he
conceives himself as having started as a "minute historian" of the

Of this rededication, the most dramatic example is Stuart P. Sherman, one-time editor of a minor Elizabethan dramatist and contributor to *Modern Language Notes, Publications of the Modern Language Association,* and *Materialen zur Kunde des älteren ënglischen Dramas,* and finally editor of the New York *Herald Tribune* "Books." The divagations that he pursued in the interim—his "coming out" for the humanism of Irving Babbitt and Paul Elmer More, his championship of Puritanism and Democracy as the bases of the American genius, his long service in education and academic administration, his decision to leave his watch-tower at the University of Illinois and immerse himself in the electric currents of life in the metropolis—these do not concern us here, however much they reveal of the problems of contemporary criticism.[6] What

literary history of the past and become a "roving critic" of the literary history of the present, without undergoing any essential change: "Being so occupied with history, that is, with things already done, Mr. Van Doren has almost no interest in the metaphysics of criticism. . . . He sets forth the patterns which he believes he has found in his subjects of investigation as if they were any other contribution to knowledge." Having a "native disposition to overlook deficiency in art for the sake of abundance of vitality," he has made what he terms "the creed of vitality" the center of his journalistic criticism. See p. 173, below.

[6] They may be viewed in detail in LIFE AND LETTERS OF STUART P. SHERMAN, 2 vols. (1929), by Jacob Zeitlin and Homer Woodbridge,

does concern us is the conception of criticism in
CRITICAL WOODCUTS, a collection of essays from
"Books," in which Sherman sets forth the creed of
the historical journalist, the historian of the present.
After dismissing his own inconsistencies with something of Emerson's jauntiness, he boldly maintains
that his primary task is reportorial:

> The first duty of a commentator on current literature, as
> it appears to me, is to present a fairly full and veracious
> report of what is going on. . . . His first duty is not to
> exploit his own predilections; it is rather to understand the
> entire "conspiracy" of forces involved in the taste of his
> own day. What is "important" now and never may be so
> again has a charm for him which he would think it a kind
> of baseness and disloyalty not to admit and record

Here we have a creed which, *mutatis mutandis,* is
identical with that of the historical scholar. Like
the scholar, he is to narrate history, to be thorough
and accurate ("full and veracious"), to subdue rather
than cultivate the personal equation, to understand
and explain rather than judge, to demonstrate what
is important in its time, to respond to the charm of
the present as the antiquarian responds to that of

a valuable contribution to the study of American literature of the
twentieth century and a stimulating book for readers trying to work
toward a critical position.

the past. Like the scholar, he gazes, fascinated, upon the flowing stream of Time:

He conceives of literature perhaps as a river, himself as a scout seeking for the main channel of intellectual and emotional activity in his own tract of time, recurring constantly to the point where the full rush of living waters comes in from the past, and eagerly searching for the point where the flood breaks out of the backwater and through the dams, and streams away into the future. He is always sounding and essaying to discover where the water is deepest now. He tries to characterize the most promising navigators, their crafts, their cargoes. When he concerns himself with historical figures, he seizes upon those who by reason of some vital congruity, are felt by us as "modern" and pertinent to our present occasions.[7]

Recalling that in his earlier criticism he has said much of "the good life," Sherman goes on to declare, in terms which the scientific scholar would readily comprehend, that a true vision of the good life is obscured by "too much theory about it and too many preoccupations," for "The best criticism is of a concrete and inductive habit. The wise critic attempts on all possible occasions to keep his theoretical and didactic mouth shut and all his other faculties open, here, there, and everywhere, for all the reports and rumors of positive charm and joy

[7] CRITICAL WOODCUTS, p. xii. A second collection of essays from "Books" was appropriately named THE MAIN STREAM.

in things and people, as the most indubitable tokens that they are participators in some degree of that 'good life' which he is seeking." Through open-minded exploration of this sort, he has learned that "patient search usually discovers some refreshing virtue wherever there has been exhibited any un-usual display of energy"—though this may be, he presently acknowledges, merely a "blind faith."

In the book thus prefaced, Sherman turns out to be less the observer who sees his subjects steadily and whole, than the advocate or optimist bent upon making a case for them. At times he goes so far that his appreciation is indistinguishable from the ordinary publisher's "blurb," as when he declares that Don Marquis's THE DARK HOURS "should affect us as the tragedies of Æschylus and Sophocles affected the Greeks." [8] One of the most deliberately composed woodcuts is the one placed first in the volume, "an introduction to the works of Mr. An-derson for the benefit of correspondents who inquire: 'When will the country begin to sicken of this flood of literary rot from the corn and hog belt?'" As advocate or optimist, Sherman proves himself able

[8] Thus in "Books"; in CRITICAL WOODCUTS he modified the affirma-tion, not too happily, by adding the word "religiously." LIFE AND LETTERS, II, 711.

to stomach all of Sherwood Anderson's faults and shortcomings, regarding which he is silent, and dilates upon his six distinguished gifts. One of these is his fine workmanship, illustrated by the first chapter, only four pages long, of DARK LAUGHTER, "as consummate a work of art as the first chapter of PRIDE AND PREJUDICE, which also occupies four pages; and the rest of the book is keyed up to that pitch." Another gift is that "he is tremendously American and glad of it." Another is that "he possesses 'high seriousness'." Still another is that he is "a genuine mystic," comparable with the author of the VITA NUOVA and the DIVINE COMEDY—works to which Sherman owes, as he candidly tells us, his ability to understand "this ex-advertising man from Chicago." Laudation of this sort, heralded at the time as proof of Sherman's insight and tolerance and courage, is incomparably more absurd than Lord Jeffrey's famous attack on Wordsworth's "Excursion" beginning "This will never do"—an assertion supported with strong arguments. Equivalent laudation Sherman bestowed upon Sinclair Lewis, Theodore Dreiser, and indeed upon the realistic-naturalistic movement of the 1920's as a whole. As he declared in his address before the American Academy of Arts and

Letters, he had the privilege of living in an age
"full of men and women bent on exploring and
reporting the truth, . . . great areas of repressed
truth about their own lives and about the lives of
the American people." We may find our keenest
pleasure, he cried warmly, in "recognizing and ap-
plauding the various aspects of the great literary
movement which is taking place under our eyes,
giving us on the whole the stimulating sense that
ours is one of the valorous and encouraging ages of
the world." Had he not met his premature death
shortly after this celebration of a movement already
disintegrating, had he lived into the fourth and fifth
decades of the century, he might have pronounced
the twenties not merely vital but also superficial and
found a later time one of the valorous and encouraging ages of the world, for his whole cast of mind
had become enthusiastically contemporaneous. He
lived in history; he lived with history. Whereas the
academic literary historian, professing to be purely
scientific, inherits the ideas of a romantic past, a
journalistic historian like Sherman, professing to be
faithfully reportorial, espouses the changing ideas
of his own time, urges the validity of the forces
which successively and incessantly modify the soul
and human societies.

III

Sherman came to New York, says Dr. Canby, "as a student, to establish living contacts with contemporary literature and with men and women and the typical life from which the new books were springing. As a critic and writer he came in order to reach a wider and more various range of adult minds." His aims, in other words, were to do what Dr. Canby himself was already doing and has now been doing for a decade. The typical scouting reporter of the movements of the stream of literature is Henry S. Canby, who has rounded out ten years of service as editor of the *Literary Review* and the *Saturday Review of Literature*.

Dr. Canby has more than once explained the function of a review of this sort. An offspring of the daily newspaper, the literary weekly has the task of presenting and interpreting "the news of literature." Unlike the journal of opinion, such as the *Nation* or the *New Republic*, it does not apply to the modern world a special social philosophy; its subject is literature and the backgrounds of literature, and its interpretation is liberal instead of propagandist. To be sure, the staff of editors will have individual convictions, since "men choose their philosophy according to their temperament," but their minds in the main will be flexible, and they will rely largely upon contributions from the "experts" outside—critics, scholars, and scientists, men of distinction rather than of uniform opinion.

If it is hard to assure adequate sympathies in a carefully selected small group of reviewers, it is wholly impossible in a large group, so that such a journal can only "hope to attain truth by averages as the scientists do, rather than by dogmatic edict." The review that criticizes a given book must itself be criticized by the reader—a formidable duty rendered somewhat easier by the signature of the reviewer, if the reader is fortunate enough to recognize his name and bias. As a further guarantee of neutrality, the journal must open its columns for the publication of protests and rebuttals. Instead of requiring conformity to a standard of its own, it voices the opinion of many minds, each able in its own way but often fundamentally in conflict with other minds. Instead of presenting an official judgment, it invites its readers to a battle of the wits. "The fight is in the open, we know the adversaries, and the final judgment, whether to salute a victor or condemn an imposter, is ours." This programme is said to provide, on the whole, the best means of telling the busy and uncritical public what books are worth; it makes "a liaison between the reader and his book" and promotes "education of the reading American mind." It provides the book news of the day, expert opinions of authors and their writings, and advice, direct or indirect, as to the Book-of-the-Week. A natural extension of this programme was the establishment of the Book-of-the-Month Club and similar organizations, which developed from the literary review as the literary review had developed from the newspaper.

Whether or not this is the best possible programme for a literary review, the value of the journal will finally depend upon the editor himself, who perhaps writes more of its pages than any other one person, and who in any case registers his personality and point of view in his many editorials and essays and in his choice of "expert" contributors. What, then, are the qualifications of Dr. Canby as a journalistic critic of literature?

By virtue of his academic training and his long association with the Department of English at Yale, Dr. Canby has a command of the history of literature incomparably superior to that of the ordinary journalist. He is familiar with the scholar —a scientist "ruthless in his accuracy, a stickler for intellectual discipline, a man like Browning's grammarian, wanting to know, no end to the knowing." He is familiar with the achievements of the scholar, as when he says, "Yes, we have settled Hoti's business (and a side-street affair it has proved): it is time to take up Pindar and Æschylus and the life and art for which Hoti was made." And if he himself does not take up Pindar and Æschylus, he does something else that he reproaches the professors for not doing: he remembers that the continuity of literary history includes the twentieth century and accordingly reads the new books and studies the trends of literature in the present. In knowledge of contemporary letters Dr. Canby has perhaps no equal in America today.

In estimating the value of contemporary letters, he deliberately avoids what he terms a "fundamental" criticism, that "austerer" criticism which always insists upon the best. For, as he avers, "In the year in which we live—and it is sometimes necessary to remind the austerer critic that we always live in the present—there are a hundred books, of poetry, of essays, of fiction, which are by no means of the first rank and yet are highly important, if only as news of what the world, in our present, is thinking and feeling. They cannot be judged, all of them, on

the top plane of perfect excellence; and if we judge
them all on any other plane, good, better, best get
inextricably mixed." In other words, the aim of
the journalist in the field of books is to give readers
the news, news less superficial than that recorded in
the newspapers, news that may be profoundly interesting to readers now even if dull hereafter. For
there are books as well as people of importance in
their own day, and one must know them if one is
to be fully alive. The prime duty of the journalist
it would perhaps be better to term not literary criticism but "literary definition."

In DEFINITIONS (1922) Dr. Canby explained:
"I use definition in no pedantic sense. I mean, in
general, logical definition where the class or *genus*
of the thing to be described—whether best-selling
novel or sentimental tendency—is first made clear,
and then its *differentia,* its differences from the type
analyzed and assorted." What this means he made
plainer in DEFINITIONS, SECOND SERIES (1924),
when he asserted that the critic's task is "to name
what our authors are doing" (whether the typical
get-rich-quick story, romantic narrative, naturalistic
novel, etc.), and then, accepting the *genre,* taking
the author on his own terms, to consider "the success or failure of what he himself has actually set

out to accomplish." [9]   In case the critic frowns upon naturalism, that fact is his private and otherwise irrelevant concern, for "if a man sets out to do naturalism, by the laws of naturalism let him be judged." The same must be said of the types within naturalism: "If, instead of drawing Tom Jones or Mr. Pickwick, it is the submerged personality of a neurotic woman that interests the writer," we must allow the writer his interest and ask only whether he has succeeded in his aim—"the thing can certainly be done, and it is certainly neither more nor less worth doing." As a definer, the critic is concerned with all the types that writers choose to cultivate, not only those in high repute, such as the ambitious novel that invites the supreme tests, but also those whose standing is inferior, such as the novel intended only to yield a pleasant hour.

For example, suppose that we judge on the highest plane IF WINTER COMES.

It fails miserably. For Mr. Hutchinson stacks the cards. He gives his hero his way and his salvation, after much suffering, by a series of lucky accidents. He destroys the problem he creates, by forging an answer. But this novel should not be judged on the highest plane. It is not

[9] Superficially, this appears to repeat the theory of Croce. The basis, however, is the *genre,* which Croce condemns as academic and unreal.

a tragedy, it is a romance. It belongs to the plane below, the plane of stories told to meet the secret desires of humanity, which have little to do with reality, and are quite oblivious to fact. On this plane IF WINTER COMES ranks highly, for it is poignantly told, there is life in its characters, and truth in the best of its scenes. Definition saves us from calling a good novel great; it spares us the unnecessary error of calling a good and readable story bad because it is not a triumph of consistent art.

Let the critic of contemporary letters be content, therefore, "to set books upon their planes and assort them into their categories. . . . This is elementary work, which may lead the critic only to the threshold" of criticism, but it is the most useful thing he can do in a time when serious criticism is unheard in "the irresponsible hullabaloo of commercial appreciation," a time when publishers with their blurbs confuse all standards and hack reviewers indulge in wholesale, superlative praise and dispraise.

This process of definition is also historical. In a suggestive passage Dr. Canby observes:

In any given moment at least three phases of literary time exist side by side. There is past time continued and bearing with it the thought and imagination of the last era, in which, in a literary sense, many readers have their only beings. . . . There is also, of course, present time, especially in the upper currents of contemporary literature which are hurried and ruffled by the events of the day, the prejudices, emotions, and interest of the moment. . . . And again there is time which, if not literally future, is future in its realization. In this future tense are being written the formative works which will become current literature only when they and the books they influence are read so widely as to become an integral part of civilization.

Turbid indeed is the "steady flow" of the river of literature, and to distinguish its constituent waters the critic must know the recent past, sympathize with the present, and even define the near future. Movements, like single books, call for definition. "When the current of taste of some new generation that overflows conventions and washes forward, or backward, into regions long unlaved, is viewed as a current, its direction plotted, its force estimated, its quality compared, why that is definition." Elsewhere Dr. Canby employs fluid metaphors drawn from biology, as when he speaks of "that area of literature in which blood runs warmly today," or of "the growing tissue where the sap is running now. That part of the literary tree may not be the most perfect, but at every present moment it is important, for there *our* life is stirring, there is the point at which we are living between the future and the past." Like many other modernists, Dr. Canby also speaks of "vigor," or "vitality," of "the impulse of the age," as if these were in themselves excellent, as when he says, "It is no crime to be romantic—it is a virtue, if that is the impulse of the age," or, "Apparently we have needed a strong dose of psychological realism (we are nearly cured) and got it, which proves neither that psychological novels are better than any other kind nor that the critics are wrong in recommending them." At bottom, his theory is simply that of historical relativity or indifferentism.

His practice, however, is often inconsistent with his theory. Employing the loose and abrupt accent of modern speech, revealing a mind acute, provocative, astute in tactics, fertile in ideas, Dr. Canby occasionally writes editorials and essays that transcend his too-modest theory. Writing on "The Young Romantics," for example, he points out that "waste has always been the romantic vice—waste of emotion, waste of words, the waste that comes from easy profusion of sentiment and the formlessness that permits it." Romantics, new style, like the author of MAIN STREET, have a vision strained and aslant, a horrid fascination by the ugly, so that "the things that these writers love in life often they never reach until the last chapter, and about them they have little to say, being exhausted by earlier virulence"—a remark worthy of Dr. Johnson's conversation. In another passage Dr. Canby commends to modern creative writers an equivalent of his own art of definition, as a remedy for vague objectives. "Many modern novels of the better class," he observes, "and a great many modern poems, seem to me awash and wallowing like derelicts on the high seas. They are successful enough in this, excellent in that, but they get nowhere, because the writers had felt the emotion that made them, or suffered the experience, but never defined it in terms of all emotion, all experience, never considered its end. The three dots . . . of modern literature are significant." In a similar vein he declares that "art, which must interpret, must therefore be coherent, whatever may be the superficial appearance of life. It is true that the coherence of life is only a hypothesis, but it is a hypothesis concomitant with the existence of man as a rational and self-respecting being, and art, if it is to be human, must support the theory." This is why, in another essay, to quote one more passage, Dr. Canby occasionally finds it necessary to survey his flowing river from a great height:

> Those who seek literary consolation are by no means to be urged away from their own literature, which contains a perfect picture of our feverish times, and has implicit

within it the medicine for our ills, if they are curable. But they may be advised to go again and more often than is now the fashion to the writings of those men who found, for their own time, a real significance, who could formulate a saving doctrine, and who could give to literature what it chiefly lacks today, a core of ethical conviction and a view of man in his world *sub specie æternitatis.* It is the appointed time in which to read Dante and Milton, Shakespeare, and Goethe, above all Plato and the great tragedies of Greece.

In such passages the editor of the *Saturday Review* shows himself more the humanist than was the editor of "Books," though he has never stayed to formulate his theory of the writer as a rational and self-respecting being in the manner in which he has formulated his theory of the writer as a creature of the flux.

If Dr. Canby ever and again reveals a pungent common sense, a direct insight, and even a certain humane elevation, together with a capacity for composition firm and shapely, it must be admitted that most of his writing suffers from both his prevailing theory and his too-strenuous practice. If it is true, as he maintains, that journalism "killed" Sherman, it has for the most part kept Dr. Canby on the plane of the superficial in thought and slipshod in word. The journalistic critic at his best cannot

undertake editorial and other duties but must bring
to focus all of his energies: like Sainte-Beuve, who,
describing his secluded mode of life, said, "I leave
the house only from necessity, to look for books—
for fodder, as I say. My whole life is spent reading, then writing, then correcting proofs." There
were long, uninterrupted hours, day after day, in
which Sainte-Beuve could reflect as well as read and
write; he was free of those irrelevant pressures that
keep thought in fragments and render composition,
whether of thought or words, experimental and premature. Now, Dr. Canby himself complains that
ours is an age without meditation, and therefore
without steady insight. Ours is the age of outlook,
even in our psychology. "The literary plants we
grow," he continues, "are brave, bright-colored fellows, fluttering with vivid details and hung with fat
fruits of philosophy. Yet now and then one longs
for some less sappy, stalky vegetables, for something
with *roots*, deep roots that go down and down into
the deep earth of long meditation." He could not
have better described what we miss in his own brave
literary plants.

In a time of intellectual and artistic chaos, when
the central need is that of constructive thought re-
sisting the disintegrating forces everywhere at work,

the journalistic critic cannot afford to limit himself to the task of intelligent reporting. That will accomplish something, perhaps, and is justified if the critic lacks the power of sending down deep roots. Something may also be accomplished by a weekly review that perforce ignores all but a comparatively few books among the thousands that pour from the presses, although it is doubtful whether a review which is virtually an open forum, making the inexpert reader the judge of the conflicting expert writers, can shape opinion so effectively as a journal that adopts a definite policy. From the choice of such an editorial policy, and from the attempt to formulate standards for the governance of his own criticism, Dr. Canby is effectively withheld by his theory of historical necessity. Loth to interfere in the least with the push of movements, he apparently assumes that movements are the work not of men but of mysterious unhuman forces. He shares very largely the modern respect—shall we say superstitious veneration?—for the "forces" that are "vital" in any given age and that demand a virtually unconditional surrender of artists and critics. The river of literature ceases to be a mere analogy or symbol; it becomes a conception nearly as rigid as that of organic evolution. Excellence is the result of a sort

[103]

of natural selection, rather than artificial or human selection. The mind of the modernist is deterministic to such an extent that, when he has casually ventured to assert himself, he looks back upon his antics with a crestfallen apathy.

As the impressionist critic cannot transcend his impressions, so the historical critic cannot transcend history. Instead of surveying and defining the stream of things from a superior vantage point, he turns out to be in fact swimming with the current—and shooting Niagara.

CHAPTER FOUR

HISTORY : PROPHECY

Here the theme is creative and has vista.
— *Walt Whitman*

WHILE USUALLY restricting himself in his common-sense way to the news and interpretation of the present, Dr. Canby often has in mind "the probable course of evolution" and on one occasion ventures to assert that "criticism is prophecy implied or direct." Yet on the whole he leaves to others that fascinated gaze into the future which he terms, in telephonic idiom, long-distance prophecy. Historical criticism becomes long-distance prophecy in the writings of such men as Randolph Bourne, Van Wyck Brooks, and Lewis Mumford, who, even when dealing with the past and the present, are never historians in the ordinary sense but idealists viewing past and present in the light of a fairer future. They are not the scholars or the reporters but the adventurers of Time. They display a fine romantic hatred of convention, whether that of the dull practical life

established by the pioneers or the equally dull
genteel tradition supported by the professors. They
enjoy an enthusiasm like that kindled by the war in
a few imaginative professors who cried: "All may
be prophets now, for the air is electric with the
promise of the new world that is to come from this
travail of nations. America never again can be what
she was before 1914. A new future opens, and
today we demand with Whitman a school of
prophets, seers, poets, interpreters of the new vision
of America among the nations." [1] Their chief an-
cestor, indeed, is Walt Whitman, whose romantic
nationalism and utopianism they repeat in terms
sobered by the scientific environmentalism of the
school of Taine.

I

The leader of this group of national culturists, as
they might be termed, was Randolph Bourne, whose
untimely death at the age of thirty-two almost made
of him a spiritual symbol. In turn of mind he was
not wholly unlike some of the self-appointed states-
men of the war, such as Henry Ford, who was re-
ported as saying, "I don't read history. That's in

[1] Fred Lewis Pattee, "Americanism through American Literature," *Educational Review*, April, 1919.

the past, I'm thinking of the future." Bourne was always thinking of the future, dreaming the long, long thoughts of youth, ardent to band Young America in a phalanx that should lead the way to a rational society. In the words of his admirer Mr. Brooks, he gave himself to a "beautiful desire . . . for a new fellowship in the youth of America as the principle of a great and revolutionary departure in our life, a league of youth, one might call it, consciously framed with the purpose of creating, out of the blind chaos of American society, a fine, free, articulate cultural order. . . . *Place aux jeunes* might have been his motto: he seemed indeed the flying wedge of the younger generation itself. . . . He was a wanderer, the child of some nation yet unborn, smitten with an inappeasable nostalgia for the Beloved Community on the far side of social-ism." That this beautiful desire sprang up in him before the war is proved by a charmingly immature book published in 1913—YOUTH AND LIFE, in which he announced in the brave accent of the poets of Vagabondia, "It is the glory of the present age that in it one can be young. . . . A muddle of a world and a wide outlook combine to inspire us to the bravest of radicalisms." In it were chapters on "The Adventure of Life," "The Experimental

[107]

Life," "The Dodging of Pressures" (conventions), and "On Radicals." In chapters bearing on science and religion he drew light from such writers of the day as Maeterlinck and Burroughs, and from Walt Whitman. It is clear to him that science "brings us only to an 'area of our dwelling,' as Whitman says. The moral adventure of the rising generation will be to learn this truth thoroughly, and to reinstate ideals and personality at the heart of the world."

Today Bourne is known, when known at all, mainly through a posthumous volume edited by Mr. Brooks, HISTORY OF A LITERARY RADICAL AND OTHER ESSAYS (1920), composed of papers already published in periodicals. In the title essay Bourne tells of his reaction against the professors ("The professors knew some history, but what did that history mean?"); of his emancipation by a lecturer who came to the village, a literary radical albeit a professor, William Lyon Phelps; of his humanitarian passion for "social purpose"; of his increasing clearness of outlook in the years following college and an architectural course; and particularly of his perception of the need of critics intent not upon "crusades against puritanism and philistinism" but upon "a constructive pointing of the way." In another essay, taking as a point of departure the vicious effects in America of Matthew Arnold's conception of culture, he describes in vigorous language "Our Cultural Humility." Misguided young Americans of talent went the way of Henry James and the bourgeoisie imitated them as best they might. But this humility, this parasitic attraction to the civilizations of Europe, he declares is "the chief obstacle which prevents us from producing any true indigenous culture of our own. I am far from saying, of course, that it is not necessary for our arts to be fertilized by the civilizations of other nations past and present. The culture of Europe has arisen only from such an extensive cross-fertilization in the past. But we have passed through that period of learning, and it is time for us now to set up our individual standards." It is time for us now, he goes on, to cultivate "a new American nationalism," based upon "the beauties and vitalities and sincerities of our own life and ideals." We are now ready to stride forward in the spirit that animated MacDowell in music, James in philosophy, and Walt Whitman in poetry. We are now ready to "shut ourselves in with our own genius" and to "express the soul of this hot chaos of America." [2]

[2] Later, disillusionment brought on by the war caused Bourne to reject this "weary old nationalism" and to envisage a "new and

II

The ardent confusion of Bourne became a thoughtful earnestness in his disciple Van Wyck Brooks, who attracted much attention in the decade 1915–1925 through a succession of studies of the malady and the promise of American letters: AMERICA'S COMING-OF-AGE (1915), LETTERS AND LEADERSHIP (1918), THE ORDEAL OF MARK TWAIN (1919), and THE PILGRIMAGE OF HENRY JAMES (1925). It will suffice to consider here only the first of these books, which reached a second printing in 1924 and is probably the most original and influential of the series.

The germ of AMERICA'S COMING-OF-AGE lies in a sentence quoted from Emerson: "Our people have their intellectual culture from one country and their duties from another." The American people, as Mr. Brooks conceives, are Highbrows and Lowbrows, drifting chaotically between the two extremes of dessicated culture and stark utility, powerless to effect that organic reconciliation of theory and practice which would turn their life into a "disinterested adventure." The absorbing adventure of business

more adventurous ideal": a cosmopolitan culture, or "federated ideal," to be worked out in the future in this land of many races. "Trans-National America."

is only the habitual prolongation of an impulse legitimate in the age of pioneering but now become a vicious anachronism. The prevailing class, having attained relative economic freedom, can find no outlet for personality save by continuing its economic self-assertion and spending its wealth in "doing what everybody else does, and doing it as much more so as possible." In simple truth it appears that "economic self-assertion still remains to most Americans a sort of moral obligation; while self-fulfillment still looks like a pretty word for selfishness." Self-fulfillment, of a sort, there was in that Golden Age when we produced Emerson, Lowell, Holmes, Whittier, and the rest of "Our Poets," who reflected a certain coherence and ripeness in our culture. Yet the vague idealism of the American people was never allowed to interfere with practical life. Not one of the New England writers was able "to move the soul of America from the accumulation of dollars"—not even Emerson, the saintly and the shrewd, the voice of German transcendental idealism and of American pioneer enterprise. "For if the logical result of a thorough-going, self-reliant individualism in the world of the spirit is to become a saint, it is no less true that the logical result of a thorough-going, self-reliant individualism in the world of the flesh is to become a millionaire." In Lowell, it may seem, the elements of personality were richer and better fused; yet he, of all our writers, was farthest from self-fulfillment "because his culture is European without the corresponding pressure and responsibility of the European mind." With the passing of Lowell and Emerson and the rest, that innocent old America came to an end, and a new and chaotic America—the hot chaos of Bourne—soon took its place. Self-fulfillment, as a social ideal, is still to seek.

That ideal is the opposite of our economic self-assertion. We must act upon our knowledge that a relative competence in worldly goods satisfies the person who is primarily and sincerely aiming at "the fulfilling of his own creative instincts,"—the working out of his own personality in terms of activity artistic, religious, and literary. Rightly viewed, these forms of activity are not, like self-assertion in the practical realm, selfish, but in the best sense social, essentially disinterested. Yet they will always be thwarted unless they are also social in the sense that they pervade society, since "the individual whose personal end varies too greatly from the end of the mass of men about him not only suffers acutely and becomes abnormal, he actually cannot accomplish anything healthily fine at all. . . . The mind is a flower that has an organic connection with the soil it springs from." Once this creative ideal prevailed, it would close up the violent antinomy that cleaves asunder American society—on the one hand the largely feminine public devoted to theory and culture and Maeterlinck, on the other the largely masculine public devoted to action and business and the dollar. At present our two publics are, "in biological phrase, infertile with one another."

One sound clue to self-realization we possess in a poet capable of mediating between the two American publics—Walt Whitman. He it was who first revealed to us something organic in our life, linking the cloud-castles of Emerson, Hawthorne, and Poe to the solid earth. "Himself a great vegetable of a man," he had nearly as large a power of gathering human experience as Ulysses of old. "Whitman—how else can I express it?—precipitated the American character. All those things which had been separate, self-sufficient, incoördinate—action, theory, idealism, business—he cast into a crucible; and they emerged, harmonious and molten, in a fresh democratic ideal, which is based on the whole personality." He was the focal center for America, as Virgil for Rome. And he points the way for us to

[113]

attain a place in the sun really worth having. Are we not to take the raw materials of his social ideal, which he shaped in the form of emotion, and reshape them, as he failed to do, in the form of guiding ideas?

If Van Wyck Brooks leaves his high theme at this point, it is partly because of his earnest modesty, which suggests to him that "the formulation of a social ideal can only be the work of a wiser head and a riper heart than we have yet seen." In 1915 he was, indeed, but twenty-nine years old, scarcely ready to make good Whitman's shortcomings in the realm of ideas. Yet he has never since become ready. As one of his disciples, Waldo Frank, has pointed out,[3] the author of AMERICA'S COMING-OF-AGE soon appeared to be "flinching from the way of which he was the intellectual leader. THE ORDEAL OF MARK TWAIN reveals the defeatist note. His distortions of portraiture no longer have the dynamic end of recreating our literary figures into forces for an American ethos: more and more, they become rationales of failure. With THE PILGRIMAGE OF HENRY JAMES a petulant delight in pain comes into his writings. The still later study of Emerson is a mere sentimental retrospect." One remembers his

[3] In THE RE-DISCOVERY OF AMERICA (1929), p. 321.

own phrase, "The mind is a flower," and the delicate flowers that bloomed in the efflorescence of
Romanticism, when Chatterton was a symbol of the
poet in conflict with society. Perhaps Mr. Brooks
himself remembers the romantics when he some-
where remarks that "to feel oneself a 'victim' is in
itself not to be an artist, for it is the nature of the
artist to live, not in the world of which he is an
effect, but in the world of which he is the cause."
But while Mr. Brooks has often analyzed the American artist as effect, he has never pictured the American artist as cause. Why is it that his doctrine of
the free creative life is paralyzed by a prevailing
mood of wistfulness and futility?

In quest of an answer, let us return to "the professors," who are mentioned in the first sentence of
AMERICA'S COMING-OF-AGE and are never afterward
out of mind. The professors conceive that literature is a thing of the past; they want that creative
spirit which is appropriate to literary studies and
essential in the ideal of self-fulfillment. Mr. Brooks
deals with them in a more sustained manner in one
of the best-known of his later essays, a contribution
to The Dial in 1918, "On Creating a Usable Past."
While the anarchy of American life and letters in-
creases, the professors, apparently in complete indif-

ference, "continue to pour out a stream of historical
works repeating the same points of view to such an
astonishing degree that they have placed a sort of
Talmudic seal upon the American tradition." Vic-
tims of their environment and training, they interpret all learning with reference not to the creative
but to the practical life; passively submitting to the
forces that starve the imagination, they fulfill themselves only in "the vicarious world of the dead" and
return to the world of the present "in the majestic
raiment of borrowed immortalities," disparaging
almost everything that issues from the contemporary mind. Instead of fertilizing the present,
they take a pathological delight in shaming the present by the example of the past. As a preparation
for "the reinterpretation of our literature" Mr.
Brooks accordingly welcomes "the reinterpretation
of our professors that now goes merrily forward."
European professors, suffering less from inhibitions,
viewing the past through the spectacles of their own
intellectual freedom, lay before the practising
author a more available body of inherited experience. For a more usable American past, we shall
have to rely upon the historical enterprise of our
younger generation. Theirs it must be to select,
from an inexhaustible storehouse of inherited experi-

ence, attitudes and ideals really pertinent to our
needs today; theirs it must be to *create* a usable
past. They will recall that Sainte-Beuve, when
Arnold objected that Lamartine was not an important writer, rejoined, "Perhaps not, but he is important *for us.*" They will ask, first of all, *What
is important for us?* And this will turn their attention from the obvious masterpieces of American literature to the "tendencies" that explain our failures.
"Why did Ambrose Bierce go wrong? Why did
Stephen Crane fail to acclimatize the modern
method in fiction twenty years ago? What became
of Herman Melville?" Would not answers to a
"hundred and one questions of this sort" enable us
to "throw an entirely new face not only over the
past but over the present and the future also?"
Would not understanding of the obstacles met by
our writers in the past link us in brotherhood with
those writers and thus offer a basis for "a national
culture"?

Yet surely, as a prophet of a national culture, Mr.
Brooks does not carry us very far. He is not much
more creative than the professors. The task he
proposes belongs, as he acknowledges, to the literary
historian. Defeated in his efforts at constructive
prophecy, he turns to the past; and he turns to the

past, not for permanent values essential for a reconstruction, as the humanist does, but merely for explanation of tendencies, as the historical professor does. He too wants to be an historical professor, only a really good one.

In this aim, he has no choice. For if American literary history is a matter of "historic destiny," and if the professorial mind is likewise "historically predestined," and if the same is true, as he tells us, of the revolt of the younger generation against the professors, so is it true, presumably, of his own mission to lead that revolt toward a more penetrating mode of research. Longing for a better literature in the future, he urges a reinterpretation of American literature in the past.[4] He has the usual academic preoccupation with conditions and tendencies, with concepts of nationality and history, with the relativities of place and time, along with the usual academic atrophy of the higher critical faculty by a deterministic view of life. AMERICA'S COMING-OF-AGE draws to a close not with a call for courage and energy but with a rueful admission that "to be a

[4] A book on THE REINTERPRETATION OF AMERICAN LITERATURE (1928) represents an effort of the professors themselves (a group of members of the Modern Language Association and a member of the American Historical Association) to undertake the task proposed by Mr. Brooks a decade earlier.

[118]

sheer determinist is in all probability to have behind one the authority of the intellect," wherefore the best that men can do is to convince themselves that "what nature wills is what they will," as "one of the greatest of determinists," Walt Whitman, understood:

> All forces have been steadily employed to complete and delight me.

It is a limp faith. What a faith more strenuous might have done for Mr. Brooks can only be imagined.

III

Several years before the publication of AMERICA'S COMING-OF-AGE, a youth of seventeen named Lewis Mumford, a son of Whitman's fish-shaped Paumanok, planned a book on utopias. Though Mr. Mumford does not indicate how he came upon the idea, he acknowledges that he would perhaps never have either started or finished writing the book but for the encouragement of Van Wyck Brooks. THE STORY OF UTOPIAS, published in 1922, expresses the post-war disillusion with the present, looks with hope into the future, and yet, significantly, is in the main a history of the utopias of the past, from Plato's REPUBLIC onward. The author distinguishes two types: utopias of escape or compensation, and utopias of reconstruction. Utopias of escape are aimless, leaving the external world unchanged; utopias of reconstruction are purposive, seeking to shape the world to the heart's desire. In a concluding chapter he calls for a reconstruction of our twentieth-century world, beginning with our inner world. Owing to the disintegration of our idola, "our mental world will soon be as empty of useful furniture as a deserted house." He finds no cheer in the reformers and revolutionaries, because of "their lack of any fundamental programme and their inability to conceive an essential reorientation in modern society." His own effort in this direction, however, is sketched in only a few pages and is obviously futile: the basis of the new order should be the elements of "consensus among all utopian writers" and its conditions should be the "limitations of each region" and the "driving force of history."

In his next two books Mr. Mumford, instead of working out a fundamental programme, studied the conditions of Utopia in a definite region and time of history—America and her brief past. In the first, STICKS AND STONES (1924), he found an index of American life in our architecture; in the second, THE GOLDEN DAY (1926), in our imaginative literature and philosophy. Since they are closely parallel in thought and the second book is far superior in firmness of conception and harmony of style, we may here limit ourselves to THE GOLDEN DAY.

The keynote of this suggestive work of historical interpretation is struck in the first sentence: "The settlement of America had its origins in the unsettlement of Europe"—i. e., in the breakup of mediæval culture. The end of one culture and the beginning of another may be symbolized by the belfries and campaniles that began to be erected all over Europe in the thirteenth century; "the bells tolled, and the idea of time, or rather, temporality, resumed its hold over men's minds." By the fifteenth century new devices in map-making rendered it possible for even ordinary men to travel to distant lands. "The bells tolled, and the ships set sail": "time and space took possession of the European's mind." Later, Protestantism, commercial expansion, and science; still later, the industrial revolution, political democracy, and utilitarianism carried forward the externalization of human interests. In America, the European was turned into a barbarian by pioneering, a romanticism of action. "The vast gap between the hope of the Romantic Movement and the reality of the pioneer period is one of the most sardonic jests of history. On one side, the bucolic innocence of the Eighteenth Century, its belief in a fresh start, and its attempt to achieve a new culture. And over against it, the epic march of the covered wagon, leaving behind it deserted villages, bleak cities, depleted soils, and the sick and exhausted souls that engraved their epitaphs in Mr. Masters' SPOON RIVER ANTHOLOGY." Instead of leading to a new culture, the breakup of mediæval culture finally produced that dehumanized, mechanistic civilization in which we now live.

But there was one golden day—Mr. Brooks's Golden Age of New England. There the inherited mediæval civilization had indeed become a shell, "but, drying up, it left behind a sweet acrid aroma, and for a brief day it had a more intense existence in the spirit. Before the life itself collapsed, men felt the full weight of it in their imagination. In the act of passing away, the Puritan begot the Transcendentalist, and the will-to-power . . . gave way to the will-to-perfection." At least "they fathomed the possibilities, these Americans, of a modern basis for culture." The leader of these minds, the Morning Star of the Golden Day, was Emerson, who summed up all that was salutary in the experience of America when he wrote in the frontier accent, "People wish to be settled: only as far as they are unsettled is there any hope for them." His challenge was met by Thoreau, the Dawn of the new day, who made a resolute attempt at self-fulfillment, and by Whitman, its High Noon.

Walt Whitman becomes the hero of this historical novel. In him the New England culture produced "poetry of the first rank," poetry indeed that belongs to "sacred literature." He it was who most fully realized a fatal lack in the humanistic and religious traditions from which the Romantic Movement had cut loose, a lack, in his own words, of "the invisible roots, the profoundest meanings, of a place, race, or nationality." Immersing himself in his environment, "Whitman absorbed so much of the America about him, that he is more than a single writer: he is almost a literature." Whereas Longfellow could be removed from our heritage without altering in the least the "possibility of American life," the removal of Whitman would result in an impoverishment of our resources, inasmuch as he "created a new pattern of experience and character." Unhappily, we have made scant use of that pattern: "the work he conceived still remains to be done: the America he evoked does not as yet exist." That is why Mr. Mumford must write his book.

[123]

The remainder of the argument I must summarize in few words. After Whitman comes the Twilight of Hawthorne and Melville, then the Civil War and its train of consequences making for a blatant industrialism instead of a finer culture. Each of the literary figures of the post-bellum period was more or less frustrated; Mark Twain, Bierce, Howells, Henry James, William James, all are the fragments of a man, till at length Mr. Dreiser illustrates only too plainly "the bewildered chaos of the sons of the pioneer." If Transcendentalism, as Emerson said, had resulted in a headache, the pragmatism of the ensuing period brought on a paralysis. A writer must either, like Henry James, flee from this pragmatic environment, or, like his brother William, accept it and glorify it. Culture itself, to this practical America after the war, became acquisitive and predatory—not something based upon experience, but something that might be purchased by those who have the means, like Mrs. Jack Gardner's palace in Boston. Our own generation, even more than the disabled generation following the Civil War, is pathetically impotent in the creative life.

Like Van Wyck Brooks, Mr. Mumford has written a fresh and thoughful study in literary history

viewed against a background of general history.[5]
Like Mr. Brooks, and unlike the usual academic
historian, he is always thinking of the future, even
though he says little about it till he reaches his
"Envoi." And here his vision, like Mr. Brooks's,
wavers uneasily between a deterministic respect for
forces and a pioneering zest for free *adventure*.
Sometimes he announces, after the manner of those
spiritual pioneers, the Transcendentalists, that "man
is not merely a poor creature, wryly adjusting himself to external circumstances: he is also a creator,
an artist, making circumstances conform to the aims
and necessities he himself freely imposes"; that the
incomparable adventure our generation may know
is to create, in lieu of the Machine philosophy since
Descartes, a philosophy oriented towards Life—
nothing less than "to conceive a new world. *'Allons!
the road is before us!'* "[6] At other times Mr. Mum-

[5] In the *American Historical Review* for October, 1927, the book
was described as "not always the kind of thing a historian would
approve, but everywhere pricking the historian into the painful
task of thinking about history"—high praise, when one considers
how rare thinking is in historical scholarship, both literary and
general.

[6] This slogan—the last words of the book—is fittingly repeated
from Walt Whitman. In a later book, HERMAN MELVILLE (1929),
Whitman and Melville are presented as our two leaders, "Whitman with his cosmic faith and Melville in his cosmic defiance."
Fused into one, they will guide us to a splendid future (p. 364).

ford, as a son of Taine, is impressed, rather, with
"the forces that have come over from the past," "the
forces that are now dominant," "the forces . . . at
large in the world." At such times, naturally, the
task of the critic is not so much to create a new
world as to arrive at a "prophecy of a new stream
of tendency." Yet it can scarcely be said that Mr.
Mumford ever arrives at any definite prophecy or
describes the prospect that makes him feel adventurous. Looking into the future "tenderly, wist-
fully, impotently," "all dressed up, with no place to
go" (as he says of instrumentalism), he might just
as well have ended his book with the disconsolate
cry: *"Impasse! the road is closed!"*

For a careful reading of his book shows, I think,
that the forces make the adventuring delusive, and
purposeful foresight impossible. At bottom, creative thought turns out to be receptive thought, its
mission being merely to gather "all the living sources
of its day" and express them. The important thing
for a writer is not a certain independence from time
and place (those two factors in experience that
brought on pioneering and pragmatism) but a full
absorption, like Whitman's, of the vital forces of his
own time and place. All the leading writers of the
Golden Age had an adventurous spirit which, para-

doxically enough, illustrates this dependence: "that the past was merely provisional, and that the future might be formed afresh were two patent generalizations which they drew directly from their environment." John Dewey's philosophy of experimentalism, similarly indebted, "expresses . . . American experience." The prevailing thought of Mr. Mumford appears to be that, in the relation of the individual to his time and place—"the perpetual intercourse between the organism and its environment"— the formative agent is the time-and-place not the individual, the environment not the organism. His most insistent questions are always biological: What recent forces are still vigorously *alive?* What new forces are gaining in *vitality?* His most insistent fear is that of a culture which is "pressed flowers" instead of a "living plant."

This accounts for his covert attacks upon the humanists, those "academic philosophers, whose chief glory it is to make bread out of straw," who ignore the life round them in their revival of cultural values that are moribund or obsolete, and who ought to bestow their encomiums forever upon William Dean Howells, faithful observer of the "inner check." Mr. Mumford does not think much of the doctrine of the inner check: "Sooner throttle a babe in its cradle than nurse an unacted desire," he rejoins with William Blake. There are limits, to be sure, to his taste for sheer vitality, since he cannot stomach Theodore Dreiser's indifference to "direction or purpose or humane standards," but he is plainly hostile to the particular direction, purpose, and standards of the group of critics called humanists, who exclude not only the realists and naturalists but also the romanticists with whom Mr. Mumford is deeply allied. Indeed, the humanists "wage war upon all the living forces of the last century"; they are not "in living relation to the important issues of their time," as Whitman and Taine were; they are not even aware that Walt Whitman himself was "a far better humanist" than Irving Babbitt.[7] Like an orthodox romanticist, Mr. Mumford condemns the humanists for "their fear of 'expansiveness,' their distrust of spiritual audacity, their high regard for correctness, their curious belief in restraint as the ultimate ethical principle,"—qualities which he ascribes, in conformity with the deterministic side of his theory, to their "academic environment." But Mr. Mumford himself has for a number of years been part of the academic environment: his books have been admired by many instructors and young

[7] *New Republic*, August 29, 1928, p. 51.

writers in the colleges, as well as by earnest minds
outside, and I think it could be shown that his work
in the third decade of the twentieth century contributed not a little to the strength of the academic
humanist position at the beginning of the fourth
decade. For, on the one hand, he has argued well
the need of a humanistic reconstruction; and on the
other, he has failed to offer any tangible reconstruction which might rival that of the humanists.

Like the humanists, he points out that we can
escape from the sterility and despair of our contemporary world only by "reformulating a more
vital tissue of ideas and symbols to supplant . . .
the abstract framework of ideas which we have used,
in lieu of a full culture, these last few centuries."
Science has achieved its astonishing results "by treating men's central interests and desires as negligible,
ignoring the fact that science itself was but a mode
of man's activity as a living creature, and that its
effort to cancel out the human element was only a
very ingenious human expedient." Though itself an
instrument of man's humanism, science has a point
of view sharply contrasting with that of humanism.
"In the 'Phaedrus,'" the author of THE STORY OF
UTOPIAS reminds us, "Socrates had expressed the
humanist outlook by saying: 'Trees and fields, you

know, cannot teach me anything, but men in the city can.' The shortest way of describing the attitude of science is to say that it resolutely turned its back on men in the city and devoted itself to the trees and fields and stars and the rest of brute nature. If it paid attention to men at all it saw them—if we may abuse an old quotation—as trees walking." Far from sharing "the scientific distrust of 'values,'" far from resting content with an humanitarian "diffusion of existing values," Mr. Mumford presents himself as the champion of higher values than those of the present—values to be created in the future with the help of the past. This he makes clearest, perhaps, in a passage in STICKS AND STONES, where he sums up the task of culture by saying that "the future of our civilization depends upon our ability to select and control our heritage from the past, to alter our present attitudes and habits, and to project fresh forms into which our energies may be freely poured." So far as the past is concerned, this means that we must have that "ability to re-introduce old elements" which "the humanists of the late Middle Ages" displayed when they restored the letters and monuments of Rome and Greece. A reinterpretation of the past is essential if we are to "bring into the foreground those things that have been left out

[130]

of the current scheme of life and thought." Both
Mr. Mumford and Mr. Brooks agree with their
humanist contemporaries in insisting upon the quest
of a usable past, even if they disagree as to what
past is usable.

Through a creative use of the past we may transcend the limits of the present and approximate a
"complete and symmetrical life." Here again Mr.
Mumford is fully in accord with the humanists,
though less explicit than they in regard to the elements of such a life—less explicit, indeed, than the
Victorian humanist Arnold, whose CULTURE AND
ANARCHY is the prototype of STICKS AND STONES
and THE GOLDEN DAY. A narrow scrutiny of the
ideal of completeness might have led him to perceive, with the humanists, the need of the comple-
mentary ideal of centrality to control and shape the
elements entering into completeness, an ideal that
Arnold illustrated in his life but that he left nearly
meaningless in his account of a capacity for *relating*
his "powers of life." Like the humanists, Mr.
Mumford urges the search for "the good life," an
old phrase that he employs constantly but never in
the derisive manner of some of the impressionists;
but what he means by it no man can certainly say.
Though deploring the "tedious war-cries and the

[131]

empty party labels" of the humanists, he himself, as a national culturist and adventurous determinist, employs a like number of terms and phrases, including not a few that the humanists have found serviceable, such as *culture, values, experience, completeness, the good life, symmetrical, heritage, humanizing,* more sparingly *humanism* and once only, I think, *humane discipline.* He has helped to accustom the contemporary ear to such terms, and, using them in blurred senses, has left to the humanists the task of bringing them nearer a focus. While commending a flexible response to the pressures of the age and the national genius, he has shown himself capable of asserting, like the humanist who refuses to compromise in respect to first principles, that at times "it is necessary to be as stiff as a ramrod and as dogmatic as a Scotch dominie." In sum, it may be said that Mr. Mumford has contributed not a little spade-work "Towards a Humanist Synthesis."[8]

[8] The title of one of his essays in the old *Freeman*, March 2, 1921. Unlike the humanists, however, he here prophesies an organic synthesis to be attained by science: "The social sciences will lie beneath the foundations of the New Jerusalem precisely in the fashion that the physical sciences now underlie the stony exterior of New York." To this faith Mr. Mumford still clings in 1930, as may be seen in his vague contribution to THE CRITIQUE OF HUMANISM. A more enlightening statement of his present relation to the humanist movement will be found in his review of

And his associate, Van Wyck Brooks, has done the
same. A harsher critic of Our Poets, Mr. Brooks
has gone so far as to tax Whitman with having
no ideas and being satisfied to have none: "He was
too complacent. He was incapable of discipline and
he did not see that discipline is, for Americans, the
condition of all forward movement." Instead of
inveighing against party-cries, labels, and the like,
Mr. Brooks announces: "It may as well be understood that the human race will have catchwords and
will not budge without them," the only question
being "whether they really *catch* at the bottom of
things." He calls upon our critical minds to "formulate new issues that really are issues," issues, that
is, lying within our social life and requiring discovery. And once the critic has selected his issues
with conviction, he must support his view of them
militantly. In a somewhat surprising passage Mr.
Brooks declares roundly: "A point of view in criticism, criticism in the genuine sense, is a working-
plan, a definition of issues, which at once renders it
impossible to make one's peace with the world, at

HUMANISM AND AMERICA in *The New Republic* for March 26, 1930.
My own view of the stand taken by Mr. Mumford and his asso-
ciates I have published in a review of THE CRITIQUE OF HUMANISM
in *The New Freeman* for June 4, 1930.

once and permanently sets one at odds with the world, inevitably makes the critic a champion and a man of war." To urge the claims of a definite programme, as Carlyle, Ruskin, Mazzini, Taine, and Nietzsche did, is no less than "the condition of life in the intellectual and moral world."

Pursuing this unexpected turn given to the doctrine of Vitality, we may well doubt whether Mr. Brooks and Mr. Mumford have themselves fulfilled the condition of life. They have never championed a definite programme, or even attained a definite point of view, though it is abundantly plain that they are at odds with the world. Making society responsible for the creative impotence of artists and critics, they sometimes seem well content merely to dream like Thoreau (as described by Mr. Mumford) the vision of a whole human life, or to long to swoon away like Emerson (as described by Mr. Brooks), who "felt as if he had drunk the soma-juice with the morning-moving deities of the Rig-Veda, as if life were all an eternal resource and a long tomorrow." At other times their wistfulness takes the more active form of romantic adventure. "Allah," says Mr. Brooks, "never counted the time the Arab spent in the chase." " '*Allons!*' " cries Mr. Mumford, " 'the road is before us' "—the road that invites the American caravan into the desert.[9]

---

[9] THE AMERICAN CARAVAN, which set off belatedly in 1927, was led not by a single *Raïs* but four editors, including Messrs. Brooks and Mumford. In THE SECOND AMERICAN CARAVAN (dedicated to Bourne) and THE NEW AMERICAN CARAVAN (dedicated to Van Wyck Brooks) there were but three editors, Mr. Brooks's name having disappeared from the title-page.

CHAPTER FIVE

HUMANISM IN THE TWEN-
TIETH CENTURY

What a piece of work is a man! How noble in reason!
how infinite in faculty!—*Shakespeare*

The just man does not permit the several elements
within him to interfere with one another, or any of them to
do the work of others,—he sets in order his own inner life,
and is his own master and his own law, and at peace with
himself.—*Plato*

And in the things that touch upon the Gods,
'Tis best in word or deed
To shun unholy pride.

—Sophocles

WALT WHITMAN was the last of the commanding personalities in American criticism of the
romantic age. His death coincided not only with
the passing of the frontier, but also with the arrival
of the Revolt of the Nineties, a movement which,
despite its debt to him, inaugurated a realism hostile
to the essentials of his creed. Through writers like
Hamlin Garland, Stephen Crane, Edwin Arling-

ton Robinson, Frank Norris, and Edith Wharton, all of whom published significant work before the end of the nineties, the realism of the early twentieth century clearly announced itself. In verse this realism received full expression, in the years following 1912, through the "New Poetry" of Amy Lowell, Robert Frost, Vachel Lindsay, Edgar Lee Masters, Carl Sandburg, and many others; and when this bewildering chorus gradually subsided after 1916, the realistic programme was continued by a large number of prose writers, including Theodore Dreiser, Sherwood Anderson, and Sinclair Lewis. This energetic creative impulse was accompanied by a critical movement antagonistic to the romanticism of the nineteenth century and sympathetic with the aims of realism; criticism more and more became (to use its own big words) impressionistic, expressionistic, sociological, and psychological.

The critical revolt first plainly declared itself in 1913—the time of the poetic revival—in a book entitled THE SPIRIT OF AMERICAN LITERATURE. The author pronounced America to be not a democracy but "a vast bourgeoisie"; depreciated its "household poet" Longfellow as "third-rate"; exalted Mark Twain and Walt Whitman; found such realists as Howells and James fine but tame and

thin; complained that American writers as a whole
are "idealistic, sweet, delicate, nicely finished" and
"turn their backs on life, miss its intensities, its significance"; conceived that "the whole country is
crying out for those who will record it, satirize it,
chant it"; and joined the American Spirit in calling upon the Muses for "twelve novelists, ten poets,
and eight dramatists, to be delivered at the earliest
possible moment." [1] In the welter of speculation
that quickly ensued, the central issue was the problem of an American culture, a problem that had
been posed in the eighteenth century and discussed
with intermittent vehemence through the nineteenth
century. Whitman pointed out that America had
achieved political independence in the eighteenth
century and economic independence in the nine-

---

[1] After John Macy, some of the critics who rose to prominence
were Van Wyck Brooks, Randolph Bourne, H. L. Mencken, Stuart
P. Sherman, Carl Van Doren, Henry S. Canby, Lewis Mumford,
and Harold E. Stearns, certain of whom performed valuable service
through their powers of unhampered observation or refreshing
satire. Although some of the foregoing critics differed widely from
one another, a number were sufficiently like-minded to find a place
among the Thirty Americans who in 1922 surveyed CIVILIZATION
IN THE UNITED STATES. In more recent years a host of critics and
biographers have sought to forward, through books and the journals
of opinion, the reinterpretation of American life and letters in
terms of modern thought, doubting almost everything except modern thought—in some cases that as well.

teenth, but that her cultural independence lay in the future. In the half-century after DEMOCRATIC VISTAS this higher independence appeared no nearer attainment; indeed, the war with Germany, while rendering America foremost in the world in respect to political and economic power, only accentuated the impotence of her culture. It is not surprising that our intellectuals, young and old, should feel that the immemorial problem of a native cultural tradition has acquired a certain urgency, and that they should be making strenuous efforts to solve it.

One cannot but doubt, however, whether the majority of our critics are likely to fare better than Whitman, inasmuch as their approach to the problem is essentially his. Like Whitman, they are living in the present (that is, the recent past) and looking into a blank future. If few of them will hazard the rôle of the prophetic critic, nearly all are contemporary critics—eager to maintain the open mind, quick to seize upon what seems most attractive and hopeful at the moment. Like Whitman, nearly all of them are in revolt against a past that they do not really know, often do not in the least care to know: their vital memories, for the most part, stop with Whitman himself, behind whom the past is a dim otherness and vast irrelevance.

Revolting against romanticism and frontier crudity, they are actually dealing with the problem of an American culture and literature, to a large extent, in the romantic and frontier spirit. They are more interested in the national "genius" than in the broadly human; they affect self-reliance rather than reliance upon the experience of the past; they are impelled by a mood of adventure more than by a will to reform with the aid of old standards. They keep in the foreground of their minds the desire for national individuality, that desire, typical of the nineteenth century, which everywhere found expression in literature based upon the national experience and in politics based upon the theory of the national state. They still ignore, almost as patently as our post-Revolutionary patriots, the fact that a national culture is a slow growth and cannot be improvised in a century or two. They still ignore the fact that America has never been shut off from the rest of the world, as the old nations substantially were, and that the multiplying mechanisms of communication have rendered solitary development hereafter impossible. They are still unable to realize that the national soul cannot be asserted but must be suffered to assert itself. They are still unable to realize that, while it would be interesting for us to be American, it is far more important for us to be human, and that while we cannot know how to become American, we can know reasonably well how to become human.

Whitman himself, as these contemporary critics fail to remember, more and more came to understand that our proper task is not one of rejection and isolation, but one of acceptance and assimilation. Even in his first Preface he mitigated his burial of the dead past with his declaration that, through evolution, the past lived in the present. By 1881, however, he came to feel that this declaration did not adequately state the bond of past and present, Europe and America. Whether because of deeper insight or, as he suggested, because of the altered vision of old age and invalidism, he was compelled to restate the matter as follows:

> Years ago I thought Americans ought to strike out separate, and have expressions of their own in highest literature. I think so still, and more decidedly than ever. But those convictions are now strongly temper'd by some additional points. . . . I see that this world of the West [America], as part of all, fuses inseparably with the East [Europe], and with all, as time does—the ever new yet old, old human race—"the same subject continued," as the novels of our grandfathers had it for chapter-heads. If we are not to hospitably receive and complete the inaugu-

rations of the old civilizations, and change their small scale
to the largest, broadest scale, what on earth are we for?

In a later passage of the same essay, pursuing the
idea of hospitable reception, Whitman frankly suggested that perhaps the best thing we can do is "to
saturate ourselves with, and continue to give imi-
tations, yet awhile, of the æsthetic models, supplies,
of that past and of those lands we spring from,"
not merely England, but in addition "stately and
devout Spain, courteous France, profound Germany, the manly Scandinavian lands, Italy's art
race, and always the mystic Orient." [2] The next
year, upon the death of Longfellow, Whitman
wrote in praise of him as the type of poet—poet of
gentle humanity—needed for self-assertive modern

---

[2] "Poetry Today in America," PROSE WORKS, II, pp. 212, 228. He
gave the same advice repeatedly. Holding that we have relied
too exclusively upon England, he urged, on one occasion, a reception of Spanish culture ("The Spanish Element in Our Nationality,"
II, pp. 116-19) and on two occasions a reception of the culture of
"all former lands" from India and Greece to Italy, France, and
Spain. ("British Literature," II, pp. 274-77; "Little or Nothing
New, After All," II, p. 296.)

Of these lands we are "inextricably the heirs." While there are
national differences, the story of mankind, Whitman repeats, is
ever "the same subject continued"—"the same old humanity—the
same old heart and brain." More and more he looked, in the
manner of Matthew Arnold, for correctives to offset national
exaggeration and to render possible a more representative humanity.

America, and endorsed "what I have heard Longfellow himself say, that were the New World to be
worthily original, and announce herself and her own
heroes, she must be well saturated with the originality of others, and respectfully consider the
heroes that lived before Agamemnon." If it ever
occurred to him to apply this unflinchingly to himself, Whitman may well have questioned whether
his own work was, after all, worthily original,
whether he had sufficiently saturated himself with
the originality of the European writers of the past.[3]
The same doubt might well be entertained today
by not a few of our most prominent creative and
critical writers, who have perhaps not even im-
mersed themselves, as Whitman did, in the King
James Bible and in Shakespeare. They have scant
inclination to heed his warning against a smart and
superficial modernity, his demand that we use
"hourly" the heritage of the past, and his reminder
that "at present, and doubtless long ahead, a certain
humility would well become us."

[3] Possibly this doubt found voice in the following passage in
A BACKWARD GLANCE: "Modern science and democracy seem'd to be
throwing out their challenge to poetry to put them in its statements
in contradistinction to the songs and myths of the past. As I see
it now (perhaps too late), I have unwittingly taken up that challenge and made an attempt at such statements—which I certainly
would not assume to do now, knowing more clearly what it means."

Now, this humility is out of the question until we face in all candor the fact that independence of the past is forever delusive. Nothing is more certain than the law of continuity, by virtue of which an age loosely termed revolutionary derives its formative ideas from the age previous. The great revolution at the close of the eighteenth century, for example, manifested in the political realm by the French Revolution and in the intellectual and artistic realm by the Romantic Movement, not only reacted against certain interests of the eighteenth century, but also cultivated other interests and brought them to fruition. Thus, a poem like "Tintern Abbey," while indeed profoundly original, was the result of more than a century of rational sensationalism; and when Emerson in NATURE sought to enjoy an original relation with the universe, he actually effected a complex interweaving of Platonism, deism, and German idealism. The same continuity might be readily illustrated in any department of human activity in any period of history. And along with continuity we must reckon also with the perennial tendency of thought to return upon itself by reviving ideas and values long neglected. The Renaissance revived elements of ancient humanism, the Romantic Movement revived elements of the Middle Ages and the Renaissance. To recur to the examples above, Wordsworth's verse harks back to Milton and Shakespeare and the ballads, Emerson drew heavily upon Plato and the Cambridge Platonists, and Whitman derived hints for his "free" verse from the rhythmical patterns of the English Bible. Through continuity and revivalism, the past is inescapable.

This is obvious. But the obvious is sometimes curiously ignored, and it is surely one of the more modest functions of criticism to perceive the obvious, and if necessary point it out to creative writers elate in their contemporaneity. Nothing is more necessary today, in this age that prides itself upon its superiority to the past even while its faith in progress is faltering, than that we should ask ourselves, in the honest, rational manner that we affect, what past we are actually using, and whether that past contains all that we need.

I

The past we are actually using, the past that has shaped our current conception of man and the universe, is the age of naturism that stretches from the seventeenth century to the present. On the far side of this age lie the faith of the Reformation, the humanism of the Renaissance, the faith of the Middle Ages, and the humanism of ancient Rome and Greece: more than twenty centuries of experience, containing virtually all the greatest figures in literature. On the near side of the seventeenth century lie the rationalism and skepticism of the epoch before the French Revolution, the aspiring emotionalism of the Romantic Movement, and the rationalism and skepticism of the nineteenth and early twentieth centuries: less than three centuries of experience, expressed in a literature fascinating in its variety but tending to the incomplete and tangential rather than to wholeness and centrality. The present is the issue of this comparatively recent past.

Although, strictly speaking, no movement can well be said to have had a beginning, it may assist our thought if we will follow Huxley in dating our modern time from an inconspicuous event in 1645—the holding of meetings in London by a few students desirous of "improving natural knowledge." For this obscure inception of the Royal Society was the proximate beginning of a movement destined, says Huxley, not only to confer immense practical benefits on men, but also to effect "a revolution in their conceptions of the universe and of themselves" and to alter profoundly "their modes of thinking and their views of right and wrong." [4] Before the close of that century, science had made vast strides, notably through the genius of Newton, and philosophy had undertaken a fresh start in the rationalism of Descartes, Hobbes, and Locke, followed early in the next century by the elegant sentimentalism of Shaftesbury. It became clear to the intellectuals of the eighteenth century that a supernatural revelation of religious or ethical truth was superfluous, that the physical universe itself was a perfect revelation of God, and that man was naturally good and perfectible. Rationalism and sentimentalism, cool analysis and enthusiastic feeling—these were divergent manifestations of the same tendency, an extraordinary faith in nature. The way was thus prepared for the great literary apostle of nature, Rousseau, who employed in her service the weapons of both abstract logic and a vehement and contagious en-

[4] For an admirable characterization of seventeenth-century currents of thought, in relation to literature, see Edwin Greenlaw's lecture on "The New Science and English Literature in the Seventeenth Century" (*Johns Hopkins Alumni Magazine,* XIII, 1925, pp. 331–59). The dominant tendencies are set forth as: (1) a "new realism," or sense of fact, reliance upon observation and experiment, (2) the overthrow of authority in favor of free inquiry, and (3) the growth of faith in progress, impelling men to improve their estate in the mundane world.

thusiasm; and by Rousseau the way was prepared, throughout Europe, for the Romantic Movement. Man being naturally good, his instincts right when unhindered, it was believed that evil must be the result of social institutions. It is conventions, and not natural depravity, that render actual life so ugly and unhappy and untrue, and it is through the assertion of self that man may win his due happiness and perceive beauty and truth. The inalienable dignity of man was boldly announced by the geniuses of the *Sturm und Drang,* by the Transcendental philosophy, and by the romantic schools of the several European countries and of America. In the temporal sphere sovereignty passed from kings to man, and in the spiritual sphere from God to man. Perhaps the ultimate romantic ideal has nowhere been better pictured than in Shelley's rapturous vision of the day that shall liberate men at last from "the pride of kings and priests":

> The loathsome mask has fallen, the man remains
> Sceptreless, free, uncircumscribed,—but man
> Equal, unclassed, tribeless, and nationless,
> Exempt from awe, worship, degree, the king
> Over himself.

Actual life, however, persistently refused to submit to the romantic vision of ideal life, and by ob-

struction and long postponement it at length broke
the facile optimism of the Cause of Man. Probably its main instrument was that very rationalistic
spirit which had supplied the doctrines of sentimentalism and romanticism. At first allies, rationalism and sentimentalism had drawn farther and
farther apart. Cool analysis of nature was the way
of science, enthusiastic feeling for nature the way
of romanticism. This disunion proved fatal to the
more exalted pretensions of romanticism. The dignity of man, based upon his natural desires, had
scarcely been triumphantly proclaimed when it was
disproved (so it seemed) by the natural sciences,
which proclaimed that not man but nature was sov-
ereign, that, instead of being king over himself and
over nature, man was merely one of nature's myriads
of subjects. The optimism associated with the emotional justification of the natural man passed into the
pessimism associated with the biological justification
of the natural man. From Wordsworth the way
leads, through Tennyson, to Thomas Hardy. By
means of evolutionary science, the actual overcame
the ideal, and correspondingly realism and naturalism overcame romanticism.

The fact that realism was a reaction against
romanticism must not be permitted, however, to

obscure their essential kinship. Both ranged their
forces in opposition to the humanistic and religious
traditions of the past, and when they also opposed
each other were merely engaged in civil warfare.
This internal conflict did not and could not result
in the complete victory of either side, because at
heart the two sides were in agreement. Alike they
were animated with the same purpose of placing
man in nature, the one praising his dignity in that
position, the other revealing his indignity. Their
hostility to each other, unlike their hostility to old
traditions, had an air of unreality. It is not surprising to find that realism frequently admits romantic elements, and that its progress has been
repeatedly interrupted by romantic revivals. Nor
is it surprising to find critics today, weary of the
oppressive rule of realism, calling for more romanticism, since the passage from the one to the other
is so easy: they dwell, in discord, under the same
roof.

Such is the past that we are using in our present
literature. If here in America our conscious memories stop with Whitman, our unconscious memories
stop with the foundation of the Royal Society and
the philosophy of Shaftesbury. Much of our reading public is still sentimental and romantic in its

taste, still willing to assume (at least while a pure, wholesome story is unfolding) that man is naturally good and lovely; and our more characteristic readers are professedly realistic and naturalistic, still willing to assume (at least while a veracious document is progressing) that man is naturally unaccountable and generally ugly. In either case it is assumed that man is an unitary not a dual being, that his "self" is his supreme concern, and that the creative expression of the self must not be hindered from without by convention nor from within by inhibition. This self, the only good of which we are sure, is characterized by an expansive pride and an expansive sympathy—the two coöperating virtues in the ethics of Rousseau and Whitman. A creed of this kind, said to be authenticated either by the romantic "heart" or by biological and psychological theory, is conceived as giving full play to the individual and perhaps the needful amount of protection to society.

Now, only the reactionary or fundamentalist mind, zealous in the service of a lost cause, will venture to assert that our modern scheme of man and the universe is totally false. Granting that, like all schemes that have obtained extended credence, it is partly sound and partly unsound, the critical mind in quest of enduring standards will confidently look for the positive contribution of the naturistic movement and endeavor to define that contribution. What has our accumulating naturistic tradition added to the traditions of humanism and religion?

It would be superficial to answer that it has given us an immense amount of natural knowledge, since knowledge has no "value" in itself, apart from a valuer. We must restate the question, and ask: What has man learned of value to himself? To this we may answer with assurance: he has come to feel and know, as never before, his relation with the physical universe. Judea and Greece, the sources of the older European culture, devoted themselves most effectually to realizing those aspects of man which appear to be independent of nature. It was left for modern Europe, especially since the seventeenth century, to devote itself to realizing those aspects of man which appear to be dependent upon nature. This it has done, especially in romanticism, by frankly recognizing, expressing, and exalting man's natural impulses; and, especially in science and realism, by seeking to understand and faithfully to represent these impulses. To arrive at a realization of man's naturalness, as well as his

humanity or divinity, was assuredly of high importance. We must concede that the "wisdom of the
ages"—the old established views of life—rested in
part upon ignorance. Our naturistic centuries, in
addition to their demolishment of myth and super-
stition, have done valuable service in acquainting
man intimately with the bond that exists between
him and external nature. They have thrown a flood
of light upon those natural impulses which had been
but slightly understood by an old humanism seeking
to control them and an old religion ever inclined to
extirpate them. We now perceive, as never before,
the folly of endeavoring to extirpate these natural
impulses and the magnitude of the task of control-
ling them. We are right in seeking to realize, if
not to justify, the ways of nature to man.

It is one thing to question and revise the old
established views of life; it is, however, quite another thing to abandon them without stopping to
examine their radical credentials. If the old views
rested in part upon ignorance of nature, our revolutionary views rest in part upon ignorance of the
past. While romanticism has been priding itself
upon its universal sympathy and understanding, and
scientific realism upon its honest search for truth,
both alike have failed to penetrate to the essentials

of the old views and to disengage them from the accidents. The modern world has been provincially intent upon its own special achievement and arrogantly indifferent to the achievement of the past. A curious consequence of this fact is a persistent confusion between the values derivable from naturism and the values inherited from humanism and religion. Blindly we ascribe to "nature and the language of the sense" elements of our experience that are actually the consequence of centuries of human ("unnatural") culture, inherited through books, tradition, institutions, and the like. This was the error of Wordsworth, for example, in "Tintern Abbey," though he corrected it in later years, perceiving that even in his Revolutionary ardor the past had been vital in him: "I . . . carried about me," he said,

> The experience of past ages, as, through help
> Of books and common life, it makes sure way
> To youthful minds.[5]

Sure way it makes, indeed, not alone to youthful but equally to mature minds, for it enshrines truths that perish never, central truths of life that have no witness in nature but that cannot be explained away by any philosophy of nature. When it be-

[5] "The Prelude," IX, ll. 331-37.

comes possible to define the unacknowledged debt of naturism to the experience of past ages, we shall doubtless be astonished to discover how slight the constructive power of naturism actually is, how small its contribution will be to the synthesis of the future. The need of our time can hardly be a continuance of our uncritical skepticism as to the beliefs of the past, but rather a critical skepticism as to the beliefs of the present.

II

This need is already felt. Some of the most cherished enthusiasms of the naturistic age, such as progress, romanticism, democracy, nationalism, have lost their warmth; the ultimate competence of science is questioned; realistic and naturalistic art appears to have entered upon disintegration and decadence. The great war has brought in its train a mood of disillusionment unfavorable to the reigning ideas of the century that culminated in the war, and a growing sense of the need for both social and intellectual reconstruction. The skepticism formerly applied to the wisdom of the ages is now frequently applied to the wisdom of our own age. Although much of this new skepticism is as puerile and wholesale as the old, more and more of it is drawing to the support of a genuinely critical movement that may be traced back, in this country, to Emerson and Lowell.

Emerson and Lowell were by no means wholly committed to the modern programme. Their vital memories reached far into the past, Lowell's to Dante and Emerson's to Plato. With an integrity equal to our own, they refused to accept anything on authority and submitted all tradition to free inquiry, seeking to disengage the permanent from the transitory elements in tradition and to reconcile the permanent elements with whatever appeared to be sound in the modern programme. Their task was continued by Charles Eliot Norton, and in the next generation by a number of critics and scholars who have been called "the new humanists."

> These all attend to one or another phase of the cleavage between man's way and nature's way—a dualism which, whether it cut between man and external nature, or between the "natural man" and the "spiritual man" within; whether it emphasize the "inner check" in any of its various modes, or, as against the naturalistic "education of the senses," commend to man the study of his own humane tradition, and summon him to take up the racial torch and hand it on—in any case places man's hope not upon what nature, whether within or without, may do for him, but upon his making himself more completely human.[6]

[6] CAMBRIDGE HISTORY OF AMERICAN LITERATURE, IV, p. 491.

[156]

This is a broad statement of a creed that has in recent years steadily acquired fresh adherents and fresh formulation.[7] The strength of this critical movement may be measured by the vehemence of the attacks upon it by the defenders of the old naturism. They object to the sharp clearness of the humanist creed, yet show their failure to understand it—condemning it, paradoxically, as both classical in its emphasis on form and romantic in its emphasis on imagination and also as both intellectualistic and moralistic ("puritanical"). If it is indeed all of these, it would seem to be immune from the charge which they press most violently of all: that it is rigid and narrow.

These attacks appeal to prejudices that have been fixed in our minds by naturistic modes of thought. A better way to consider the reconstruction proposed by the new humanism would be to examine its fundamental assumptions.

The first of these assumptions is that assumptions

[7] The "new humanists" named in the CAMBRIDGE HISTORY are Paul Elmer More, Irving Babbitt, John Jay Chapman, and George Edward Woodberry. To these might be added W. C. Brownell, F. J. Mather, Jr., P. H. Frye, William F. Giese, Barry Cerf, Samuel Strauss, Stuart P. Sherman (especially in his earlier work), Robert Shafer, P. H. Houston, G. R. Elliott, and younger men whose names are less familiar.

are inevitable, since every conception of life ultimately rests upon them. Absolute skepticism, if
there were such a thing, would rest upon the assumption that unlimited doubt is necessary, a position
that not even Anatole France was willing to take:

> I have feared those two words, full of a formidable
> sterility, "I doubt." So powerful are they that the
> mouth that has once pronounced them truly is for ever
> sealed, and can never reopen. If one doubts, one must
> keep silent; for, whatever one may discourse about, to
> speak is to affirm. Since I had not the courage for silence
> and renunciation, I willed to believe and did so. I at least
> believed in the relativity of things, and the succession of
> phenomena.[8]

Practically, silence is impossible, absolute skepticism
is impossible. Practically, we live by belief, by
faith, by that which we provisionally *know:* that
which appears to us most nearly to correspond with
reality, or rather with experience, or rather still
with those portions of experience that we choose to
value. Shrinking from the specter of sterility—
that everlasting No—we make our affirmations,
today no less than in the past, identifying our
belief with the truth. Of this fact few naturists in
our time seem to be aware. For the most part they

---

[8] ON LIFE AND LETTERS, Third Series, xi. So, too, Plato had taught
that a faithful sensationalism must be speechless.

dogmatically affirm that they can know and explain
man and the universe, and patiently proceed to reduce everything in experience to a deterministic
monism. In order to attain this conclusion, they
assume, first, the final validity of reason, declaring
their perfect faith in it, despite the testimony of the
history of philosophy that faith in reason may lead
to bewilderingly diverse doctrines. They therefore
assume, secondly, that the reality to be explored by
reason is the succession of phenomena, the realm
of physical science; and thirdly, that whatever experience appears to conflict with this reality must
be explained—if necessary, explained away—in
terms of this natural reality. Such are the assumptions of our current naturistic thought that prides
itself upon its avoidance of mere "faith"; such are
the assumptions that underlie the great bulk of
our so-called realistic and naturalistic literature, and
of the criticism that interprets and encourages this
literature. These assumptions we may now compare
with the further assumptions of humanism.

Humanism assumes, secondly, that the essential
elements of human experience are precisely those
which appear to conflict with the reality explored
by naturism. It recognizes, indeed, the service of
naturism: the service of romanticism in showing

the power of the natural man's impulses, the service
of biology in showing the physical union of man
with nature, the service of psychology in showing
the instinctive processes that man shares with other
forms of life; for thus has been demonstrated, if
nothing else, the magnitude of the problem of morality. Yet exactly here, in the realm of the moral
or specifically human, our modern faith is impotent.
Nature, apparently blind and pitiless, indifferent to
all that we value most, affords no light in our search
for a *modus vivendi* in a state of society. In vain
do we seek in her for standards of justice, self-
restraint, moderation, gentleness; in vain for a
principle of rational or spiritual guidance adequate
for human life as we know it. The ethical problem
cannot be illuminated by a naturistic philosophy
which merely affirms, optimistically or pessimis-
tically, that man is motivated by natural instinct,
or informs us, at best, how his moral habits may be
"explained" by the process of evolution. In the
motion picture of reality that science offers there
are no values, but only quantitative measurements of
force, mass, etc. Yet values are in fact the main
concern of man, the perennial object of his ardent
striving.[9]

[9] Science measures what are significantly called *facts,* i. e., things

Accordingly, the central assumption of humanism is that of a dualism of man and nature, as opposed to the monism assumed by naturism. Conceding, with Emerson, the possibility that the contrasting realms of the human and the natural might be reconciled if we could behold them both *ab extra*—that in the highest view the ancient maxim "Know Thyself" and the modern "Study Nature" may offer two approaches to the same reality—humanism is skeptical of all such speculation based upon the assumption of an underlying unity and is convinced that, practically, the rightful concern of man is his humanity, his world of value and quality that marks him off from a merely quantitative natural order.

In assuming this dualism, humanism appeals to the authority of the actual experience of mankind, past and present. Of the trend of past experience there can be no doubt; both of the old guiding tra-

done, phenomenal happenings viewed in retrospect. It believes that all the facts can be found, and that when they have been found, it will also be able to predict succeeding steps in evolution. These steps could then be measured quantitatively. A few less confident scientists, however, believe that, even if our knowledge of the past were complete, we could discern nothing in the past that would enable us to foresee the variations of the future. They thus point to a differentiating principle of pivotal importance, and confess their inability, as scientists, to deal with it.

ditions, the Greek and the Christian, however different outwardly, were absolutely at one in their sharp contrast between the human and the natural. Scarcely more doubtful is the trend of present experience; even in an age when the official philosophy is monistic, the working philosophy of the vast majority of mankind is still dualistic. Men are still conscious of an inner conflict, insusceptible of reconciliation, between the expression of natural desire and the will to conform to a standard of values. The failure of naturism to define new values has resulted in the continued application of the essentials of the classical and Christian traditions, even on the part of countless persons who profess the rejection of all tradition. Few indeed are those who are living "according to nature," expressing the "self" (that is, temperament) in disregard of convention without and inhibition within; most men are still living "according to society," patterning themselves in harmony with a general code and consequently restraining themselves. It is still the belief of most men (if by no means their invariable practice) that perfection is a worthy end, that it depends upon the control of the natural by the human, and that it necessitates loyalty to standards of truth and justice which cannot be con-

[162]

ceived as natural but which are none the less binding. On the one side is the inclination of nature, sufficient for the conduct of the animal creation but insufficient for the conduct of man; on the other side, the authority of conscience (which remains a fact, even when "accounted for") and the authority of the laws, written and unwritten, that give direction to the activities of the conscience. These laws are the product of the convention-making power that man incessantly exerts, in revolutionary no less than in stable ages:

> As if his whole vocation
> Were endless imitation.

Of necessity, a natural, spontaneous action is rare, since, even when only once repeated, it is already in danger of moving toward a convention or social habit. Unconventionality itself quickly becomes conventional, as one may observe, in any period, among the young or the old who cultivate emancipation from conventions that do not please them. Thus do the most natural people bear witness to their humanity.

Finally, humanism assumes the freedom of the will to conform to a standard of values, as opposed to the deterministic assumption of naturism. While acknowledging that reason leads readily to a belief in necessity, whether that necessity be spiritual or mechanical, humanism is unwilling to follow reason when it proposes a conclusion at variance with the manifest facts of experience. It is a matter of universal experience that we assume our power to will our next actions; life appears to be impossible on other terms. Common sense, as well as intuition, dictates the assumption of choice. This is the precarious but ineluctible dignity of man, clearly affirmed by Greek humanism and by Christianity, confusedly promulgated by a romanticism that lost itself in nature, and still accepted in practice by a scientific age that rejects it in theory. We may believe, like Browning's Andrea, that we are in God's hand, or, like the behaviorist, that we are in Nature's hand, and yet actually we shall proceed to carry out the actions we have determined upon, in the conviction that they represent our own free choice. While the ultimate criterion of our actions may be God or Nature, in either case we assume, along with the Victorian Tennyson, that

> Our wills are ours, to make them thine,

and along with the mediæval Dante, that

> . . . la sua volontate è nostra pace.

In judging the acts of our fellows in the intercourse

of daily life, we assume that they also are free to choose, or, as we prefer to say when their actions affect ourselves, that they are *responsible* for what they do. Our theoretical belief in the sovereignty of Providence or in the fatality of instinct and environment is forgotten in the practical experience of life.

Such have always been the assumptions of humanism. In opposition to the assumptions of naturism—first, that it makes no assumptions, secondly, that reason is the only sure guide, thirdly, that the reality found by reason consists of the phenomenal order, and fourthly, that no specifically human reality exists—humanism today, as in the past, assumes, first, that assumptions are unavoidable, secondly, that the essential reality of experience is not natural but ethical, thirdly, that there is a sharp dualism between man and nature, and fourthly, that man's will is free. Reflecting upon life in the light of these premises, humanism arrives at a doctrine and a discipline that may be briefly stated as follows:

1. An adequate human standard calls for *completeness;* it demands the cultivation of every part of human nature, including "natural" human nature. It suppresses nothing.

[165]

2. But it also calls for *proportion:* it demands the harmony of the parts with the whole. Instead of "accepting life" indiscriminately, it imposes a scale of values.

3. This complete, proportionate standard may be said to consist of the *normally or typically human.* It is concerned with the central and the universal, not the eccentric and the idiosyncratic. It is concerned with a permanently valid ethos, not with any temporary code of conventional society.

4. Although such an ethos has never existed, it has been approximated in the great ages of *the past,* to which humanism accordingly looks for guidance. It looks chiefly toward Greece, where it still finds its best examples (in sculpture, in Homer and Sophocles, in Plato and Aristotle); also toward Rome (Virgil, Horace), toward the Christian tradition (Jesus, Paul, Augustine, Francis of Assisi), toward the Orient (Buddha, Confucius), toward moderns like Shakespeare, Milton, and Goethe. Selecting the "constants" that appear to be worthy of preservation, humanism seeks to transcend the specialism that limits all ages in the past as well as the present age.

5. Unlike romanticism, which in its quest of a natural ethos repudiated the logical faculty, human-

ism is always true to its Hellenic origin in its faith in *reason*. It seeks to deal positively with the whole of experience, including those elements of experience that do not fall within the scope of what is termed science.

6. Unlike the conceptions of life that grow out of science, humanism seeks to press beyond reason by the use of *intuition* or *imagination,* following the example of the most poetical of Hellenic philosophers, who resorted again and again to symbol and myth, and the example of the foremost Christian poet when he forsook the guidance of Virgil in favor of that of Beatrice. Humanism holds that, after reason has brought us before the veil that shrouds truth, a power above the reason is needed to cope with what Goethe termed "the illusion of a higher reality." This power above the reason is the human or ethical imagination, as distinguished from the natural or pathetic imagination, which is below the reason.[10]

[10] The excellence of Greek art may be said to lie in its success in achieving unified form while suggesting an ethical infinite. The romantic critics employed an insidious flattery when they credited Greek art with executing its humanistic aim "in the utmost perfection," in contrast with modern art, which "can only do justice to its endeavors after what is infinite by approximation." (A. W. Schlegel, DRAMATIC ART AND LITERATURE, Lecture I; cf. Coleridge, WORKS, IV, p. 29, and Lowell, PROSE WORKS, IV, pp. 232–35, POETICAL

7. The ultimate ethical principle is that of *restraint* or *control*, indicated alike by practical experience and by the light of reason and the ethical imagination. There is a law for man and a law for thing. That which is law in nature becomes anarchy when surrendered to by man—the anarchy of wandering desires and blind impulses, the morbid ebb and flow of unhindered temperament, the restless oscillations of expansive pride and expansive sympathy. This anarchy is the product of romanticism and naturalism in their pure state, that is, when they do not wittingly or unwittingly draw upon the humanistic or religious tradition. As Coleridge perceived,

> The Sensual and the Dark rebel in vain,
> Slaves by their own compulsion!

Freedom and power and happiness cannot be won

WORKS, IV, pp. 45–46.) This contrast between the Greek perfection within fixed limits and the modern imperfection arising from infinite aspiration involves a twofold confusion: first, a confusion of the Christian aspiration toward the Infinite with the romantic yearning for the limitless and indefinite, the one quenching desire and the other exalting it; and secondly, a confusion of the classical aspiration toward an ethical infinite with the romantic yearning for the limitless and indefinite. The scholarship of the nineteenth century has made it clear that the Greeks, even in the "definite" forms of their sculpture, sought to express, as Professor Gardner says, an "inexhaustible idealism"—an endless approximation.

by those who practice the modern philosophy of what is loosely termed "self-expression." They can be won only when the energies of the instinctive self have been harnessed by the ethical self:

> The winged Courser, like a gen'rous Horse,
> Shows most true Mettle when you *check* his Course.

Humanism remembers, to be sure, that the Popean neo-classicists as well as the Puritans, instead of checking the steed, generally locked him in the stable, where he might indeed rebel in vain; it remembers always the need of freedom, which it defines as liberation from outer constraints and subjection to inner law. It asserts that this inner law of concentration, when it has eagerly expansive senses and emotional energies to command, is the true source of power, of character, of elevation, of happiness.[11]

[11] H. S. Canby has well described (DEFINITIONS, 1922, pp. 165–66) the "anti-Puritans" of twentieth-century literature who, assuming that all things have been proved false except their desires, make a philosophy of these desires. Their truth they derive from psychoanalysis, which they interpret to be a scientific justification of the frank expression of desires. They are quite unaware, however, that the traditional humanistic and religious values actually hold an important place in the popular books on psychotherapy. Dr. A. F. Riggs, for example, tells us that animals act "presumably without choice or without reason. On the other hand, the human being presides over the conflict of his own instincts, felt by him as a

8. This center to which humanism refers everything, this centripetal energy which counteracts the multifarious centrifugal impulses, this magnetic will which draws the flux of our sensations toward it while itself remaining at rest, is the reality that gives

conflict of emotions. He presides over this conflict with intelligence and with a consciousness of the power and necessity of choice." "It is like guiding spirited horses—you guide, they obey, not their own impulse, but your will." "It is when intelligence and will are used to realize an ideal through an action which is contrary to instinctive demands, that animal behavior rises to the dignity of human conduct." (JUST NERVES, 1922.) In another book Dr. J. A. Jackson and Helen M. Salisbury inform us that "Character is what we do with our instincts. . . . We may follow our primal desires, we may deny their existence, or we may use them for ends which are in harmony with our lives as we want them to be." "What Paul calls the law of his members warring against the law of his mind is simply what we call today the instinctive desires coming into conflict with our conscious ideal." (OUTWITTING OUR NERVES, 1922.) In a third book we may read that Jesus, the perfect man, illustrates "the right expression of power. He exerts it *over* himself, and *on behalf of* others. His self-mastery is complete, so that the claims of body and mind are acceded to or denied at will." He is contrasted with "the primitive man, whose instinctive energy pushes forth to destroy rather than to build up." (G. Coster, PSYCHOANALYSIS FOR NORMAL PEOPLE, 1926.) All of these books call to us, with the ancient Greek sage, "Know Thyself," and exhort us to conversion, which they term sublimation, and to the quest of salvation, which they term mental and physical health (*mens sana in corpore sano*). Their psychology is new, after all, chiefly in showing the power and the subtlety of that instinctive life the control of which renders man human. The humanist may be grateful for this new light on the appetitive principle in the Aristotelian ethics; the religionist, for this new light on the devil.

rise to religion. Pure humanism is content to describe it thus in physical terms, as an observed fact
of experience; it hesitates to pass beyond its experimental knowledge to the dogmatic affirmations of
any of the great religions. It cannot bring itself to
accept a formal theology (any more than it can accept a romantic idealism) that has been set up in
defiance of reason, for it holds that the value of
supernatural intuition must be tested by the intellect.
Again, it fears the asceticism to which religion tends
in consequence of a too harsh dualism of the flesh
and the spirit, for, as we have said, humanism calls
for completeness, wishing to use and not annihilate
dangerous forces. Unlike religion, it assigns an important place to the instruments of both science and
art. Nevertheless, it agrees with religion in its perception of the ethical will as a power above the ordinary self, an impersonal reality in which all men
may share despite the diversity of personal temperament and toward which their attitude must be one
of subjection. This perception, immensely strength-
ened for us by Christianity, was already present in
the humanism of the Greeks, who saw that the un-
pardonable sin is insolence or presumption, an over-
weening pride of passion or reason, a failure to be
mindful of the Nemesis that lies in wait for dispro-

[171]

portionate self-assertion. Humanism, no less than religion, enjoins the virtue of *humility*.

From what has been said, it should be clear that humanism, like Greek philosophy, "begins with science and not with religion," and that it is "a serious endeavor to understand the world and man, having for its chief aim the discovery of the right way of life and the conversion of people to it." [12]

III

The working philosophy of humanism includes an æsthetic. Though fundamentally it is the æsthetic of classicism, the modern humanist will so far as possible give it a modern statement.

Beauty may advantageously be considered with reference to quantity and quality, i.e., degree and kind.

1. *Quantity*. The æsthetic of the naturistic age, as the speculation of Benedetto Croce indicates, has tended to consider beauty only with reference to degree. According to Croce, beauty is merely perfect expression, and expression that falls short of perfection is in so far ugly. This theory is a sophisticated result of the romantic rejection of objective

[12] Such is J. Burnet's characterization of the central spirit of Greek philosophy, THE LEGACY OF GREECE, p. 58.

imitation in favor of subjective expression; we are no longer to deal with truth of imitation but only with intensity of expression. "Intensity," together with its synonym "vitality," is now in the forefront of our critical terminology. "There is a vitality which lies back both of naturalism and of romance," as a recent American critic has said; and he calls for "a fourth dimension" that will require criticism to ask of a work of art, not only Is it true? is it good? is it beautiful? but also *Is it alive?* His suggestion is gratuitous: this is the one question that naturism is eager to ask of works of art. Are they alive, vital, intense, like the works of nature; in other words, are they organic and not mechanical? Do they unfold like flowers, at the prompting of an inner urge, and so attain an inevitable form or complete expression? Or has the human agent consciously interposed his own will between Nature and her indirect product, and marred this product?

It must be admitted that the idea of the organic, which even Plato and Aristotle found useful in thinking upon art, has been carried to the point of absurdity by both romanticism and realism. It has virtually destroyed the idea of human purpose or design, which is fundamental in the æsthetic of humanism. It has caused us to suffer the delusion of thinking that selection is not a fact, when it is actually the primary fact in nearly the entire artistic process, from the initial period of preparation to the final period of revision. "Nearly the entire," we must say, rather than "the entire"; for there enters into the work of art, also, an element of the incalculable, something that appears to transcend the normal power of the artist to find what he wants. This something-given, this inspiration, may be conceived as proceeding either from the subconscious activity of nature in us or from the superconscious activity of a reality congruous with our humanity. It is conceived in the latter manner in the invocations of the classical poets and of the Christian Milton praying for divine assistance; this is the æsthetic aspect of the humility of humanism.

While avoiding the misuse of the biological analogy of the organic, the modern humanist has a sufficient sense of the importance of a vitality that permeates the whole artistic work and assures expression of all the parts that constitute the whole. In addition he has an adequate sense of the need of conscious design and selection, by means of which art, or human form-giving, is differentiated from the turbid flux of nature. He is even more solicitous than the naturist of completeness of expression, of a maximum quantity of beauty, and he believes that it can be attained, not by the identification of art and nature (the prime æsthetic heresy of modern thought), but by the employment of human powers —clear purpose, hard deliberate effort, and the insight that rewards toil.

2. *Quality.* There are not only degrees but also kinds of beauty. If there were only degrees, we should have to regard all complete, proportionate expressions as equal, regardless of the nature of the expressions; but common sense alone suffices to prove that we are inevitably concerned with the nature of the things expressed. Common sense tells us that "The Rape of the Lock" and "Paradise Lost," the "Ode to the West Wind" and KING LEAR, "On First Looking into Chapman's Homer" and the ILIAD itself are not equally admirable, even though we assume that they are all perfect expressions. The most we can say is that they are perfect expressions in their kind. We know, further, that the question of kind involves those moral and intellectual considerations that Croce seeks to rule out of art. Especially in a representative art like literature, we ask not only, How beautiful is this poem, this drama? but also, What kind of beauty does it possess? What is the worth of that which it ex-

presses? What is its truth, its goodness? Critical theory has always insisted, down to our naturistic age, upon the need of thus distinguishing between form and content, and if it has often erred by forgetting the intimate relation of the two, it has erred less seriously than our modern theory that identifies them. We cannot rest content with perfection of form; we are bound to consider also what it is that has this perfection and how it compares with other things that likewise have it. The artist selected certain materials for expression; we are to judge his selection no less than his expression.

Now, an artist may select his materials from the several great provinces of experience, namely, the senses, the feelings, the reason, and the ethical will. Since he can hardly hope to explore all of these provinces equally, he will specially interest himself in some of them and relatively neglect others. If he is a romantic, he will emphasize sense impressions and natural feeling and subordinate reason and ethical imagination. If he is a realist, he will emphasize sense observation and reason and subordinate natural feeling and ethical imagination. If he is a classicist, he will emphasize reason and ethical imagination and subordinate the senses and feelings.

This would seem to be equivalent to saying that

classicism emphasizes the more important realms of experience and subordinates the less important, and that it therefore offers the finest conception of beauty. We may miss in it the bewildering variety and indeterminateness of romantic emotionalism, together with the exquisite sense perceptions characteristic of both romanticism and realism, but, living in a naturistic age, we are perhaps not in a position plausibly to affirm that authors like Sophocles and Virgil had too little of these. However that may be, the humanist critic, prizing reason and ethical control and insight as the height of human power, must view classical art as the nearest approach to the ideal kind. Exalting what is essential, subordinating what is secondary, it approximates an all-comprehensive, duly proportioned kind of art.

In drawing this conclusion, the modern humanist must deal with the claim that primacy in kind, as well as in degree, belongs to Shakespeare. He may seek to show that the enigmatic Shakespeare was essentially a humanist, the contemporary, as it has been said, of all those who, avoiding both the natural and the supernatural, dwell upon "the wide sunlit human level" where "truth and goodness and beauty remain the same from age to age." But the annexation of Shakespeare to the humanist domain,

I think we are bound to feel, is a somewhat high-handed procedure even though partly justified. While he contributed to the humanistic ideal, he did not embody its essentials as Milton did. It is best to face the issue in all candor: to point out that Milton, the greatest English poet since Shakespeare, conceded the supremacy of the ancients; that Goethe, the greatest writer since Milton, did the same; that the claim of Shakespeare was put forward in a naturistic age, romantic critics urging it with an exaggeration that is now manifest to us; that while Shakespeare accords well with Anglo-Saxon and Teutonic predilections, he is comparatively alien to those Latin peoples whose centrality in respect to art it is difficult to deny; that—to go to the heart of the matter—Shakespeare was apparently concerned rather with mirroring life than with interpreting it, and therefore tended to submit to actuality rather than to transcend it. If his vision embraced more of life than any other author has contemplated; if he has presented, as Dr. Johnson acknowledged, "scenes from which a hermit may estimate the transactions of the world, and a confessor predict the progress of the passions," it is equally true that his works are "a forest, in which the oaks extend their branches, and pines tower in the air, interspersed sometimes with weeds and brambles, and sometimes giving shelter to myrtles and to roses; filling the eye with awful pomp, and gratifying the mind with endless diversity." He is like nature—an open secret, vast and varied, confused and enigmatic. If we must refuse to say of Sophocles that "He saw life steadily and saw it whole," it is because his tragedies do not include all of life; if we must refuse to say it of Shakespeare, it is because, though Argus-eyed, he did not see life steadily enough, did not bring his incomparably abundant materials into that order and harmony of vision that distinguishes art from experience. The image that he offers is partially blurred and elusive; his profoundest commentators, accordingly, are at variance as to his "meaning," and his lay readers find little solace in him from the apparent meaninglessness of life itself. Despite the impressive development of his mind and art, Shakespeare to the end failed to resolve his inner confusion, which limited the qualitative excellence of his art, or his corresponding outward confusion, which limited the quantitative excellence of his art.[13]

[13] Of this confusion the character of Hamlet is symbolical. More than any other tragic agent in the plays, he is critically aware of the chaos of forces that actuate "the paragon of animals."

For our best examples of sound art, which gives to ample materials firmness of inner meaning and of outward form, in other words fuses quality and quantity of beauty, we must still return to the ancients. Though we have far more knowledge than they had, though existence is to us tremendously more complex, the fact is inescapable that our materials have overwhelmed us, and that in losing control of the essentials of art we have paid an enormous price for the gains we have made in nonessentials.

In thus asserting the primacy of an art that flourished several centuries before Christ, the humanist does not, however, propose a gospel of stagnation. He gives due weight to both continuity and experiment, believes in both tradition and change.

For tradition, rightly understood, implies change; is not repetition but development; is a cumulous process in which new elements are constantly assimilated into the old structure or organism. It may be thought of as an evolution, provided that we suffer no deterministic delusions as to progress toward an unknown goal in the future, but keep our eyes steadfastly upon the humane standard envisioned by the labor of the past and inherited by the present only in so far as the present is aware of it. Tradition allows for a principle of variation, as inexplicable and inevitable as in organic science, by virtue of which each age, indeed each artist, possesses a new individuality. It welcomes the registration of this individuality, so long as the superior principle of continuity is not violated by an arrogant and artificial self-exploitation. It believes that an artist who has a valuable "originality" may safely trust that originality to take care of itself, while he can unite himself with the past in a vital manner only by dint of a humble and ardent discipline.[14] Tradition, it has been well said, "involves, in the first place, the historical sense, which we may call indispensable to any one who would continue to be a

[14] "This is especially true in the arts which we call the fine arts, where technique and tradition are of prime importance; and it would not perhaps be too fantastic to attribute, in part at least, the downfall of painting, architecture, and the handicrafts in the earlier decades of the nineteenth century—perhaps the greatest artistic disaster the world has ever suffered—to this modern enthusiasm for the originality of creative genius, and the desire on the part of every artist and architect and handicraftsman to display as conspicuously as possible his own personality and peculiar gifts. Ever since then the history of art has been the history of conscious and violent revolutions and reactions, instead of that gradual and unconscious modification of an inherited tradition which characterized its development in previous ages." (Logan Pearsall Smith, WORDS AND IDIOMS, pp. 116–117.)

[181]

poet beyond his twenty-fifth year; and the historical
sense involves a perception, not only of the pastness
of the past, but of its presence; the historical sense
compels a man to write not merely with his own
generation in his bones, but with a feeling that the
whole of the literature of Europe from Homer and
within it the whole of the literature of his own country has a simultaneous existence and composes a
simultaneous order." [15] Awareness of this simultaneous order is assuredly far more important, both
to the artist and to the critic, than awareness of that
merely successive order that Croce proposes, with
his law of an historical sequence "dominating the
dance of the intuitions." Tradition is to be conceived as a living world of achieved art, into which
the latest work will be admitted only if it is both new
and old, new because of a different angle or personal
medium, old because of its memory of time-hallowed
truth and beauty. It must give the past the power
to speak again, with a new accent. It must prove
afresh the immortality of the past, and is likely itself
to attain immortality in proportion as it enters into
the central current of tradition. If the poet is a
man speaking to men, rather than an individual expressing his idiosyncrasy, he cannot hope to address

[15] T. S. Eliot, THE SACRED WOOD, pp. 43-44.

humanity hereafter unless humanity has already addressed him; unless he is aware, as Mr. Eliot says finely, "not of what is dead, but of what is already living."

IV

The critical method of modern humanism remains to be indicated.

Its first step is historical understanding: it seeks in the beginning to remove whatever historical barrier may exist between us and a work of art. In this object it is in accord with the kind of scholarship that flourishes today everywhere, especially in the universities, a scholarship rendered possible by the historic sense that arose in the naturistic movement, which demonstrated the otherness of past ages, the operation of an *Entwickelung* linking the successive ages, and the fact that art is in some sense the product of racial heritage, environment, and the time. Through historical scholarship we are able to work our way back to past ages, to live in them like contemporaries, to read their books as they were originally read in the light of the forms and habits of the particular civilization then existing. Vividly do we see today the need of making this return, if our literary criticism is to have a substantial foundation. The great task, however, is to erect a structure upon the foundation, and from this task the humanist will not shrink as the historical critic does:

> The historical critic approaches literature as the manifestation of an evolutionary process in which all the phases are of equal value. Essentially, he has no concern with the greater or less literary excellence of the objects whose history he traces—their existence is alone sufficient for him; a bad book is as important as a good one, and much more important than a good one if it exercised, as bad books have a way of doing, a real influence on the course of literature. In practice, it is true, the historical critic generally fails of this ideal of unimpassioned objectivity. He either begins by making judgments of value for himself or accepts those judgments which have been endorsed by tradition.[16]

When true to his calling, the historical critic is not concerned with what is best irrespective of time but merely with what is fittest at the moment. He asserts that we must have complete knowledge before we can have judgment of values, thus postponing judgment to a future that can never arrive. He forgets, perhaps, that he would have no calling if humanity did not insist that literature is of value. Humanism is here, as always, with humanity; it believes that literature exists because it has value,

[16] J. Middleton Murry, ASPECTS OF LITERATURE, p. 3.

and it seeks to determine wherein that value resides.

Before judgment of value is possible, however, the critic must take a second preparatory step: he must supplement the understanding born of knowledge with the understanding born of sympathy. Holding his standards of judgment in abeyance, he must endeavor to read the book not only as if he were a contemporary of the author but as if he were the author himself. Through a more cultivated æsthetic sensibility and a fuller willingness to submit himself to the author's spirit than the erudite historian is likely to possess,[17] he will seek to reproduce in himself the author's vision, to re-create the æsthetic experience of which the book is the external expression, to revive in its totality the intention of which it is the issue. Biographical knowledge will help him, here, far less than a sympathetic release of his faculties in response to the book. He will be well aware of the fact that sympathy, like knowledge, is never complete, and that his judgments will therefore contain, like the truths of science, an element of uncertainty; but he will refuse to take refuge from uncertainty in an impressionistic self-exploitation. Having come to understand the book

[17] See the passage on erudition and critical elasticity in Arnold's ON TRANSLATING HOMER, Eversley edition, pp. 245–46.

as fully as possible, he will proceed to the specific task of criticism: judgment of the book's value.

First, its value, its beauty, considered quantitatively. He will ask, In what *degree* has the artist succeeded in carrying out his æsthetic intention? This he can answer by comparing the book, or physical work of art, with the artist's intention as revealed to him by knowledge and sympathy. If book and intention coincide, the book is entirely beautiful. If the book falls in some measure short of the æsthetic experience it was intended to represent, its beauty is to that extent imperfect. Perhaps nearly all books are in some measure imperfect, since authors, like other human beings, mar their achievement through such weaknesses as haste and laziness, halting their efforts before they have fully carried out their intention. The ugly consequences are obscurity, diffuseness, misplaced emphasis, inconsistency, cacophony, and the like. The criterion of quantitative beauty, it will be observed, is supplied not by the critic but by the artist himself, or, to be more exact, by the artist's intention.

Secondly, the critic will judge of beauty qualitatively, asking What *kind* of beauty does the book have? In answering this question, he can no longer accept without question the artist's intention, as if

one intention were as good as another. While
artists are prone to resent the questioning of their
intentions, presupposing that these intentions are
admirable and that only their success in carrying
them out is open to debate, they rarely hesitate
to question the intentions of other artists. Sin-
cerity of intention and efficiency of execution do not
constitute a sufficient test of excellence in the æsthetic
any more than in the moral realm. The critic must
test also the object itself. Is it sound or false, and
if sound, how does it compare with other sound
objects?

The criterion in this case is not the artist or the
critic but truth or nature—the nature of things,
things as they really are. This has been the aim
of all the great movements in the history of art;
they have all been professedly realistic. In its
general intention, what we term realism today
differs not at all from past art; its intention is
philosophical, it differs only in the philosophy that
it uses. That philosophy, as we have seen, finds its
master truth in the phenomenal order described by
the natural sciences, and is radically in agreement
with the romantic philosophy that delighted in sing-
ing epithalamia in celebration of the emotional union
of man and nature. Wordsworth, like the modern

realist, asserted that the object of poetry is truth, and his truth was certainly closer to the truth of the realist than to that of Aristotle, whom he cites in the same passage as having said that "Poetry is the most philosophical of all writing." The philosophy of classicism (not the pseudo-classicism that perverted the ancient doctrines and provoked the romantic revolt), while it superficially agreed with romanticism in holding that the real is the ideal, fundamentally disagreed in holding that the ideal is ethical and therefore irreconcilable with nature. The philosophy of humanism finds its master truth, not in men as they are (realism) or in men as worse than they are (naturalism) or in men as they "wish" to be (romanticism), but in men as they "ought" to be—"ought," of course, not in the usual restrictedly moral sense, but with reference to the perfection of the human type. Hence, in the words of a contemporary critic at home in both the ancient and the modern world:

> The true literary critic must have a humanistic philosophy. His inquiries must be modulated, subject to an intimate, organic governance, by an ideal of the good life. He is not the mere investigator of facts; existence is never for him synonymous with value, and it is of the utmost importance that he should never be deluded into believing that it is. He will not accept from Hegel the thesis that all

the events of human history, all man's spiritual activities, are equally authentic manifestations of Spirit; he will not even recognize the existence of Spirit. He may accept from Croce the thesis that art is the expression of intuitions, but he will not be extravagantly grateful, because his duty as a critic is to distinguish between intuitions and to decide that one is more significant than another. A philosophy of art that lends him no aid in this and affords no indication why the expression of one intuition should be preferred to the expression of another is of little value to him. He will incline to say that Hegel and Croce are the scientists of art rather than its philosophers.

Here, then, is the opposition: between the philosophy that borrows its values from science and the philosophy which shares its values with art. We may put it with more cogency and truth: the opposition lies between a philosophy without values and a philosophy based upon them. For values are human, anthropocentric. . . .

An ideal of the good life, it it is to have the internal coherence and the organic force of a true ideal, *must inevitably be æsthetic*. There is no other power than our æsthetic intuition by which we can imagine or conceive it; we can express it only in æsthetic terms. We say, for instance, the good life is that in which man has achieved a harmony of the diverse elements in his soul. . . . Plato's philosophy is æsthetic through and through, and because it is æsthetic it is the most human, the most permanently pregnant of all philosophies. Much labor has been spent on the examination of the identity which Plato established between the good and the beautiful. It is labor lost, for that identity is axiomatic, absolute, irreducible. The Greeks knew by instinct that it is so, and in their common speech the word

[189]

for a gentleman was the καλὸς κἀγαθός, the beautiful-good. . . .

It only remained for Aristotle to discern the nature of the relation between artistic "imitation" and the ideal for the Platonic system to be complete and four-square, a perpetual inspiration and an everlasting foundation for art and the criticism of art.[18]

V

Having sketched the æsthetic theory and the critical procedure of the new humanism, we may return, finally, to its practical relation with the problem of an American literature and culture. Humanism maintains that it is idle to aspire to an Americanism based upon hostility toward and ignorance of the past; that if we are ever to be worthily American we must first be worthily human; that the attainment of humanity is a task calling less for construction than for reconstruction; that the old established views of life must be revived and corrected by those who will take pains to examine the radical credentials of those views. Although such a reorientation should be sought simultaneously in all the higher departments of human activity—in philosophy, in religion, in art—it may be sought with the largest prospect of success in art, especially the

18 Murry, *op. cit.,* pp. 7–10.

art of letters. Chaotic though our literature is today, it is nevertheless more vital than either our "scientific" philosophy or our sentimental and materialistic religion. It has ample energies that might be controlled and shaped for use, instead of being diffused and lost, as at present, in tangential experiment. Unlike technical philosophy and formal religion, it already possesses an enormous, eager audience, thanks partly to the mechanical inventions of the naturistic age. A cause as well as a result, our literature is not only expressing but determining the thoughts and feelings of millions of readers.

Before a new order of creative literature can arrive, however, the way must be prepared by criticism. The modern poet or novelist who flatters himself that he is creating something new will generally be found to be following, toward the dim inane, one of the old paths marked out by his naturistic predecessors. Vaunting himself upon his individualism, his independence of all tradition and authority, he is none the less incapable of eluding the past, and a narrowly limited past at that. How, save through criticism, can he become aware of a larger, richer, deeper beauty, how else come to see the need of drawing back toward the center of life and art, how else perceive that in his quest for novelty he must carry with him the permanent and the universal and thus reconcile change with tradition? How, save through criticism, can he be provided with an audience who will understand his efforts to do something better than move toward the limbo of the eccentric, the *cul de sac* of the falsely original, and who, understanding him, will give him support and encouragement to continue more earnestly than before? Even genius of the first order doubtless needs a sensible amount of preparation, a state of the public mind that it can express and intensify; and a lesser artist is wholly dependent upon it. If such an artist today were to attempt a restoration of the pivotal values of art, he would presumably be damned with silence, or with the remark that he did not "belong" to our enlightened modern world, or with meaningless cries of "Victorian! Puritan!" He could not even count upon the support of the educators of youth, the scholars in the colleges, to whom the past is matter for historical record rather than a school of judgment. It is a deplorable fact that the young literary aspirant, whether he graduates from practical journalism or from the noisy haven of "college activities," is aware of only two possibilities of success in his art: he may be a vital realist or he may be a sophisticated romantic—in either case a little more eccentric than his predecessors.

In a recent anthology,[19] the editor points out that already "our critical spirit is prodigiously fecund." It is strenuously trying, he says, quoting Matthew Arnold, "to make an intellectual situation of which the creative power can profitably avail itself"; and this it is "actually accomplishing," he declares on his own account, not through its "actual performances or apparent direction," but simply through its "native vigor." To write thus, however, is to subscribe to the current confusion of quantity with quality. We do not need more, but better criticism, if we are to have better readers and better writers. It is difficult to see how a mere continuance and multiplication of our usual types of criticism could ever rouse from sleep this "noble and puissant nation" of ours, destined, according to the anthologist, to fulfill Milton's prophetic vision. Certainly our "apparent direction" is not toward the kind of nobility that Milton had in view, nor toward the kind of intellectual situation that Arnold desired: for we are alien from the essential doctrine and discipline that guided both the Puritan humanist and the Victorian humanist. We are naturists, and our

[19] AMERICAN CRITICISM, 1926, ed. by W. A. Drake.

[193]

criticism is historical, psychological, expressionistic, impressionistic.

Adopting the spirit and method of science, our historical and psychological critics concern themselves with description and explanation, with fact instead of value, with cause instead of result. One of our "sociological" critics, for example, is satisfied when he has shown in a study of Sherwood Anderson "how impossible it would have been for him to have written another tragedy like OTHELLO, another novel like PERSUASION; and one of our "psychoanalytical" critics restricts his function to tracing "Poe's art to an abnormal condition of the nerves and his critical ideas to a rationalized defence of the limitations of his own taste." These are ambitious tasks, they are even interesting tasks; but they do not in the least forward the central aim of criticism, which is the determination and the application of standards of value. OTHELLO and PERSUASION, the works of Poe and of Sherwood Anderson, these remain what they were: unvalued expressions. Our impressionistic critics, the followers of Anatole France, are even less helpful, dealing as they do with themselves rather than with works of art. Obedient to the romantic cult of uniqueness and to the skeptical spirit encouraged by science, they throw over the task of evaluation and with admirable candor tell us that they are interested only in self-expression, that is, in new creation rather than in criticism of what has already been created. They tell us that truth is "the adoration of second-rate men," and that they wish to be first-rate men like Carlyle and Macaulay, poor judges but great artists—"They could make the thing charming, and that is always a million times more important than making it true." These impressionists we should give leave to be as charming as they can, but for criticism we must turn elsewhere. If we turn to the expressionists, the followers of Croce, we shall find a theory useful so far as it goes. In the spirit of romanticism, they regard each work of art as a unique expression, and in the spirit of science, they measure its beauty quantitatively. In doing so, however, they endeavor, unlike the impressionists, to escape from themselves into the work of art and to judge it as the artist himself might have judged it, asking: To what extent does it express the intuition that gave it birth? This is a very sensible and pertinent question, properly the first question we must ask of a work of art. But it is not the only question. We must make bold to ask also, Is it true? Is it good? What kind of truth does it offer, and what

is its ethical quality? These are the last questions
that humanity has traditionally asked of works of
art, and we must ask them today if we are to pre-
pare an intellectual situation of which the creative
power can profitably avail itself.

"We stand today" (to quote our anthologist
once more) "in the center of a vast disintegration.
In America the situation is complicated by the peculiar problems of our own culture. Our forces and
problems must be organized before the artist can
do his work. Perhaps the reason why the creative
spirit has never (in literature) experienced a full
flowering in America, and is at present enervated
in Europe, is that the artist exhausts his creative
energy in a squandrous [*sic*] and unavailing struggle before this synthesis can be reached." No longer
is the situation in America really "peculiar." No
longer is America the only great frontier nation,
no longer is it solitary in that provincialism that
Poe and Emerson and Whitman deplored, no longer
is it alone in its severance from the vital traditions
of the past; Europe likewise has lost her moorings
and is drifting without apparent direction, although
her unconscious tradition, her profound under-cur-
rent, is far stronger than ours. Everywhere, the
need of the age is integration, the establishment of

[196]

a significant relation between the present and the past. We are sufficiently aware of the arbitrary elements in the integrations of the past; it is time for us to become aware of the arbitrary elements in our present thought that are delaying the integration of the future.

A NOTE ON HUMANISM AND RELIGION

THE SPIRIT of revolt and skepticism having reached the saturation point, more and more people are beginning to look for principles of order and construction, and humanism, because it offers such principles, is receiving more and more attention. Humanism is entering upon a new phase, not merely because of this increased attention, but also because this increased attention has for the first time necessitated a candid inspection of the fundamental issues it raises. Hostile critics can no longer hope to oppose it successfully by expressing prejudices and irrelevancies. It is no longer enough, for instance, to complain that humanism is mainly "academic" in origin, as if that proved its total depravity; nor is it any longer enough to condemn it as "Puritan" (whatever that may mean) or as Roman Catholic. Friendly critics, moreover, are now asking questions that are helpful because they are really searching. Humanism can only be grateful for the spirit in which Mr. T. S. Eliot, for example, concludes his earnest essay on "The Humanism of Irving Babbitt":

> I believe that it is better to recognize the weaknesses of humanism at once, and allow for them, so that the structure may not crash beneath an excessive weight; and so that we may arrive at an enduring recognition of its value for us, and of our obligation to its author.[1]

Certainly all humanists who share the modern critical spirit must honestly desire to recognize the weaknesses of their position. They can only be grateful, again, for the serious discussion of fundamentals in a recent essay by Mr. G. K. Chesterton. Writing on the question "Is Humanism a Religion?" [2] Mr. Chesterton affirms:

> We need a rally of the really *human* things; will which is morals, memory which is tradition, culture which is the mental thrift of our fathers. Nevertheless, my first duty is to answer the question put to me; and I must answer it in the negative.

[1] This essay on Professor Babbitt first appeared in *The Forum* in 1928 and in the same year was reprinted in FOR LANCELOT ANDREWES. After the present note was written, Mr. Eliot published in *The New Adelphi* for June, 1929, also in *The Hound and Horn* for July, 1929, "Second Thoughts About Humanism," dealing with my own account of humanism in the concluding chapter of AMERICAN CRITICISM (Chapter V in the present volume). His second thoughts being essentially the same as his first, I did not feel it necessary to alter my discussion.

[2] *The Criterion,* April, 1929; republished in the same year in a collection of essays entitled THE THING.

Though in the main friendly toward humanism, Mr. Chesterton answers the question as a Roman Catholic, and his answer acquires weight from the fact that the same desire for principles of order and construction which is interesting people in humanism is interesting them in religion. If life on the natural plane, as now abundantly appears, spells chaos, we must seek order and construction on the human plane, or on the plane above the human, or on both of these. Accordingly, no problem is more pertinent today than the relation of humanism and religion; and to that problem I wish briefly to address myself, speaking as a critical humanist.

When I say "religion," I am not mainly concerned with the great organized religions; I know too little about the professed and actual creeds of the various forms of Protestantism, or of that Anglo-Catholicism to which Mr. Eliot adheres, or of the Roman Church to which Mr. Chesterton is a convert. To all of these save certain futile forms of Protestantism, my attitude is one of respect and admiration, in so far as I understand what is essential in them. If as a critical humanist—a "pure" or "mere" humanist— I cannot avail myself of all that any of them offers, I can at least perceive that humanism and religion are in principle and in effect allied in opposition to what I have termed "naturism," the unsatisfactory programme of the Occident since the seventeenth century. Yet while I conceive that their joint hostility to the pretensions of naturism is the matter of primary importance, it seems to me that they cannot afford to neglect their relation to each other.

In discussing this relation, writers like Mr. Eliot, Mr. Chesterton, and Mr. Read appear to have raised four questions, viz.,

1. Is humanism a religion (or an alternative to religion, or auxiliary to religion)?

2. Is humanism a derivation from the Christian tradition?

3. How many people can humanism satisfy?

4. How long a time can humanism satisfy?

To the first question, Is humanism a religion? the answer is in the negative. Of the three levels of life, the natural, the human, and the superhuman, it is predominantly concerned with the second. If "the religious view" is construed in Mr. Eliot's way as requiring acceptance of "dogma or revelation," humanism certainly does not take that view. If the religious view is more freely construed as indicating a predominant concern with the level above the human, again humanism certainly does not take that view. Humanism is not a religion but a working philosophy, having for its object as a philosophy the clarification of human values, and for its object as a mode of working the realization of human values.[3] Operating in the critical rather than the dogmatic spirit, it conceives that the old religious solutions are inadequate, and it at the same time fears the delusions into which men so easily plunge when seeking to pass, without a *via media,* from the natural to the superhuman level. It agrees with one of Trollope's characters, who says: "Till we can become divine we must be content to be human, lest in our hurry

[3] Humanism is not a systematic philosophy. In answering its great question, "In what does human perfection consist?" humanism pursues not the method of philosophy in the rigid sense but rather the flexible method of culture as Arnold conceived it— "culture seeking the determination of this question through *all* the voices of human experience which have been heard upon it, of art, science, poetry, philosophy, history, as well as of religion." Only, humanism wishes to avoid the ambiguities and vaguenesses of Arnold's thought, whenever experience has proved them to be dangerous. A humanist who is content to describe religion as "morality touched with emotion" and who subscribes himself a Wordsworthian while shutting his eyes to the naturistic fundamentals in Wordsworth's working philosophy, is no longer sufficient in these more strenuous times. The twentieth-century humanist must acknowledge his debt to Arnold by defining more clearly the ideas of Arnold.

for a change we sink to something lower." It believes that there is need as well as room for a working philosophy mediating between dogma and skepticism and devoid of revelation and ecclesiastical organization.

Humanism is not a religion. It is possible, indeed, to conceive of a humanism without religion—an alternative to religion. Certainly, humanism is capable of attracting the worldly as opposed to the otherworldly, because it offers, as naturism does not, order and happiness, if not the best order and happiness. It appeals to those who can find in themselves no vocation for spiritual humility, but who do find in themselves a steadying devotion to humane proportion. As an alternative to the ideal of the religious man, humanism in this incomplete sense offers the ideal of the civilized man. This is something, it is at least far better than the barbarism that prevails in most ages, including the present.

In its complete form, however, humanism is far from disregarding religion; indeed, it may properly be conceived as including some of the essentials of religion, since it seeks to enter, under the control of the critical spirit, into the third and highest level of human experience—experience so different from the ordinary texture of life that we are inclined to speak

of it as superhuman. Though the predominant concern of humanism is with the human level, its critical
spirit apprises it of a level above the human, a higher
reality than human reason can comprehend, most
nearly glimpsed by the ethical imagination. It does
not find the second syllable of the word enthusiasm
meaningless. In its insistence on conversion (by
right habit), on the exertion of the ethical will (to
which, not to reason, it finally assigns supremacy),
on the high function of imagination, on the need of
meditation, on the need, above all, of humility, and
in its offering of substantial happiness (at its best,
an exalted peace) as the fruit of right living, humanism would seem to include much that is essential in
religion. It attracts persons who are content to be
human, but not to be worldlings.

Again, humanism may be regarded as auxiliary to
religion. It attracts not only those seeking order as
critical individualists, but also those who feel the
need of order as members of a visible church. Prot-
estantists and Catholics alike find something in it
which they either do not find in the church or which
supports what they find in the church. If it seems
to win adherents from the churches, it also seems
capable, on the other hand, of leading its adherents
into the churches. Since humanism gladly concedes

that religion is higher than a humanism devoid of religion, its more spiritually minded adherents are not always satisfied with the inevitable vagueness of religion as humanism conceives it, but wish to press on to the supreme level of life with the aid of one of the forms of revealed religion, till in time, perhaps, they are side by side with persons who were first attracted to the church and to humanism afterwards.[4]

So much for the first question. The second question is: Is humanism a derivation from the Christian religion, or, as Mr. Chesterton would have it, from the Catholic tradition? Historically, I think it will be granted, humanism has owed far less to Protestantism than to Catholicism. Humanism and Catholicism are old allies; in a general way, for instance, they may be said to have produced the illus-

[4] Mr. Chesterton distrusts religion "outside the central spiritual tradition," because it does not "last." He does not deny that it exists *while* it lasts. Mr. Eliot is more explicit, asserting that pure humanism, as I have used the term, "repudiates religion," is "*incompatible* with religious faith." If he had been still more explicit, he should have said that pure humanism is incompatible with a dogmatic, revealed religion; that is true, I think. When religion in this sense is united with humanism, the result is, literally, an "impure" humanism, or, more properly, some kind of "Christian" humanism. ("For us," says Mr. Eliot, "religion is of course Christianity.")

trious seventeenth century in France. In so far as
humanism has been nourished by Catholic doctrine,
it is Catholic. But the foundation of humanism,
"for us," as Mr. Eliot would say, is classical, is
Greek, is pre-Christian. In so far as Catholicism
has been nourished by Greek and later humanism, it
is itself humanistic. Today, at all events, humanism is not content to draw only upon Catholicism,
but rather seeks an historical justification in various
traditions antedating the foundation of the Church
—Greek, Hebraic, Buddhist, Confucian. It is by no
means content to know the first two of these through
Catholic doctrine, and, adding the last two, it may
perhaps be conceived as laying claim to universality.
The special concern of Irving Babbitt is not with
the Catholic tradition but rather with Confucianism
and Buddhism ("there is probably no one in England or America who understands early Buddhism
better than he," says Mr. Eliot), and still more with
the Greek tradition, which is scientific in the full
sense. Certainly the critical spirit, which dominates
the thought of Mr. Babbitt, and which causes him
to assert that the doctrines of humanism rest fundamentally upon present experience rather than upon
tradition, flourished incomparably in pre-Christian
Greece, the leading source of humanism whether

considered as a movement in the past or as a movement today seeking redefinition. Of the essence of humanism one may venture to say, as Paul Elmer More (whose inner history, by the way, has revolved round Plato) has said of the law of taste, that it is "less changeable than religious creeds, far less changeable than scientific theories. The advent of Christianity has left it untouched, and the waning of faith does not trouble it." Though Christianity has by no means left humanism untouched, I cannot see that it has altered it fundamentally, however valuable the deeper insight it gave into the problem of evil and the need of humility—an insight, besides, that may be had through Oriental testimony, as Mr. Babbitt has shown. I have not the slightest desire to belittle the contribution of the Christian or the Catholic tradition. The point is simply that present humanists need not accept Mr. Chesterton's dictum that humanism is "the pools" while Roman Catholicism is "the fountain." If I must name *the* fountain, I am bound to name Greek humanism: Plato, Aristotle, Phidias, Pindar, Sophocles: a fountain of perpetual youth. To the pure *humanist,* the central humanist tradition must count for more than the central spiritual tradition. While he cannot contemplate St. Francis or the author of THE IMITA-

TION without an ardor of response that superficial moderns would term benighted, he responds even more eagerly to the broadly human type represented, say, by Sophocles, not as a romantic (like Gilbert Murray) pictures him, but rather as he appears, for example, in an article by Lane Cooper:

> As a typical Greek, Sophocles is religious; not, like the Athenians in their later decadence, "too religious" as Saint Paul described them. He is also many-sided, with a number of diverse faculties ready for the accomplishment of both his immediate and his final aim. But the unity and compactness of structure in his ŒDIPUS REX or his ANTIGONE reflect the inner unity of spirit in their author. Sophocles knows when to amplify and when to inhibit; he is equally sensitive to broad perspective and to the value of each detail. His vision is steady and comprehensive, as a comparison of the eighth Psalm, in the Bible, with his chorus on man, in the ANTIGONE, will disclose. He has formed a just estimate of the relation between external nature, mankind, and the divine.

It is a matter of choice, no doubt; but the choice of the humanist is that vision of a proportioned totality, that selective comprehensiveness, that just relation of the planes or levels of life which was more nearly attained in the Greece of Pericles than in any subsequent time or place.

Two questions remain: How many people can humanism satisfy, and how long a time can it

satisfy? It may as well be stated frankly that
humanism is not centrally concerned with these questions. If it attracts persons of intellectual distinction, as Mr. Chesterton says it does, the reason is
not that it promises to reconstitute humanity. If
Mr. Babbitt "knows too much," as Mr. Eliot seems
to regret—if "he knows too many religions and
philosophies, has assimilated their spirit too thoroughly" and cannot "give himself to any," the reason is not that Mr. Babbitt wishes to satisfy all of
the people all of the time. If this *were* his purpose,
he might be expected to act upon the suggestion of a
sentence which Mr. Eliot quotes from him:

> Under certain conditions that are already partly in
> sight, the Catholic Church may perhaps be the only
> institution left in the Occident that can be counted upon
> to uphold civilized standards.

—That is, he might be expected to throw in his lot
with this majestic institution. This, as a critical
humanist, a modern seeking a sound individualism,
he cannot do. And yet, though "numbers" are not
the central concern, the humanist may be permitted
to entertain the hope of Matthew Arnold that the
saving remnant, in our large modern States, while
small relatively, may bulk large enough "to become
an actual power." The Baconians and the Rous-

seauists who have absorbed the majority were once
a small minority. Through the instinct of imitation,
through the need and desire of men for leadership,
through the many facilities for the formation of
public opinion, anything, good or bad, saving or
disrupting, has a chance to prevail. Once the remnant has reached a certain size, it will tend more and
more to set the tone of thought, of art, of education,
of life. Humanists may hope for this if they can;
they have the same right as anybody else to be opti-
mistic or pessimistic. Only they grievously err, I
think, when like Matthew Arnold they permit the
passion to "prevail" to bulk larger than their passion for perfection. In the present age at least, they
are all too likely, like Stuart P. Sherman, to drift
into humanitarianism.

No, humanists will not be unduly impressed with
the fact that Mr. Chesterton, as he reminds us,
shares his faith and his mysteries with three hundred million people. If he shared them with an
equal number of Buddhists or Christian Scientists,
that again would not centrally commend his point of
view. So that when he tells us, "I really want to
know whether it is anticipated that there will be
three hundred million Humanists," our first answer
is that humanists have more important questions to

study, and the second answer is that they deem it unwise to forecast the future. Somebody has said (I think it was Mr. Chesterton himself) that prophesying is an easy game, having no rules. But correct prophesying, a true forecast of the religion of "all the other generations . . . even unto the end of the world," Mr. Chesterton must assuredly leave to the Divine.

Mr. Chesterton speaks more pertinently when he inquires what *cement* humanism has for an enduring ethic and culture, what it possesses analogous to the aqueduct of Rome whose arches bestride lands and ages. As the past has proved, humanism allies itself naturally with dogmatic religion, so that if dogmatic religion has a future, humanism has, most probably, also. But in case dogmatic religion should continue to lapse, or wholly fail to exert a vital control over men's minds, this external cement will be wanting and humanism will have to rely entirely upon the kind of cohesion revealed by the critical spirit. The final effort of the modern or critical spirit must be to render clear and commanding an inner authority competent to take the place of outer authority. This effort has been going on for centuries now, bunglingly, because it began by throwing overboard humanism and religion along with their wrappages of authority. The next stage, as humanists conceive, ought to be the restoration and impressive clarification of all that is sound in the old traditions, all that conforms to present experience when this experience is studied far more searchingly than in the half-baked philosophies and psychologies of our professedly scientific time. Instead of beginning at the outside, with nature, humanism conceives that we must now begin with the inside, with the central facts of experience, to the end that, having examined man as an animal, we may now come to know man as man. To announce with Mr. Eliot, at this juncture, that one lays "no claim to being modern," is somewhat premature. So long as the modern or critical spirit continues to dominate men's thinking, so long will a critical humanism be justified in seeking to reveal what is really central and normal and permanent in human existence, what principles of conduct are necessary to effect a community rather than a social chaos, what kinds of knowledge and types of beauty are most congruent with human nature, what elements enter into a richly diversified, a finely shaped, and an exalted life.

READINGS

GENERAL—I. COLLECTIONS

PAYNE, WILLIAM MORTON (ed.) American Literary Criticism. 1904. [Selections, R. H. Dana to Henry James, with an historical introduction.]

LEWISOHN, LUDWIG (ed.). A Modern Book of Criticism. 1919. [Selections, French, German, English, and American, 19th and 20th centuries. The Modern Library.]

SPINGARN, J. E. (ed.). Criticism in America, Its Function and Status. 1924. [Selections from Spingarn, Woodberry, Brownell, Brooks, Babbitt, Mencken, Eliot, Sherman, Boyd.]

BOWMAN, JAMES CLOYD (ed.). Contemporary American Criticism. 1926. [Selections from 21 writers.]

DRAKE, WILLIAM A. (ed.). American Criticism, 1926. 1926. [Selections covering July, 1925–July, 1926.]

FOERSTER, NORMAN (ed.). American Critical Essays. 1930. [Selections, Poe to the present. The World's Classics.]

GENERAL—II. HISTORICAL AND CRITICAL STUDIES

FOERSTER, NORMAN. American Criticism: A Study in Literary Theory from Poe to the Present. 1928. [Contains chapters on Poe, Emerson, Lowell, Whitman, The Twentieth Century.]

SCOTT-JAMES, R. A. The Making of Literature: Some Principles of Criticism Examined in the Light of Ancient and Modern Theory. 1929. [Interpretation of the history of criticism from the Greeks to Croce.]

HUMANISM IN THE RENAISSANCE

THOMPSON, JAMES WESTFALL, George Rowley, Ferdinand Schevill,

[213]

and George Sarton. The Civilization of the Renaissance.
1929. [Brief, readable, authoritative essays on Exploration
and Discovery, Society, Science, and Art. 130 pp.]

BURCKHARDT, JACOB. The Civilization of the Renaissance. Translated from the Fifteenth German Edition by S. G. C. Middle-
more. 1929. [The standard work on the subject.]

SYMONDS, JOHN ADDINGTON. The Revival of Learning. 1877. [On
Italian Humanism, being Part II of The Renaissance in Italy.]

SPINGARN, J. E. A History of Literary Criticism in the Renaissance.
1899; revised edition, 1908.

SMITH, PRESERVED. Erasmus, A Study of His Life, Ideals, and Place
in History. 1923.

ALLEN, P. S. Erasmus' Services to Learning. n.d. [A lecture.]

PINEAU, J. B. Érasme, sa pensée religieuse. 1924.

CERF, BARRY. "Rabelais: An Appreciation." *The Romanic Review*,
VI (1915), 113-149. [A modern humanist view. For a similar
view of Montaigne see P. H. Frye, VISIONS AND CHIMERAS,
1929.]

IMPRESSIONISM

LEWISOHN, LUDWIG (ed.). A Modern Book of Criticism. 1919.
[Parts I and IV.]

FRANCE, ANATOLE. On Life and Letters. Four series, translated,
1911-24.

LEMAÎTRE, JULES. Literary Impressions. Translated by A. W.
Evans. 1921.

BRUNETIÈRE, F. B. Brunetière's Essays in French Literature. [Con-
tains an essay in opposition to "Impressionist Criticism."]

BELIS, A. La critique française. 1926. [Chapters on Brunetière,
Faguet, Lemaître, Anatole France.]

ANTONIU, ANNETTE. Anatole France, Critique littéraire. 1929.

GATES, LEWIS E. Studies and Appreciations. 1900. [Contains a
study of "Impressionism and Appreciation." The same in
American Critical Essays, ed. Norman Foerster.]

PATER, WALTER. The Renaissance. 1873. ["Preface" and "Conclusion."]

WILDE, OSCAR. Intentions. 1891.

SPINGARN, J. E. Creative Criticism. 1917. [The first essay deals with the relation of impressionistic and expressionistic criticism.]

MENCKEN, H. L. Prejudices. 1919 and after.

BOYD, ERNEST. H. L. Mencken. 1925.

———. Studies from Ten Literatures. 1925.

HISTORY—SCHOLARSHIP AND JOURNALISM

TAINE, H. A. History of English Literature. Various editions in translation. [The Introduction contains the formula.]

BABBITT, IRVING. The Masters of Modern French Criticism. 1912. [Especially the chapters on Sainte-Beuve and Taine.]

———. Literature and the American College. 1908.

FEUILLERAT, ALBERT. "Scholarship and Literary Criticism." *Yale Review*, XIV (1925), 309–324.

FOERSTER, NORMAN (ed.). The Reinterpretation of American Literature. 1928. [See the Introduction.]

———. The American Scholar: A Study in Litteræ Inhumaniores. 1929.

CAZAMIAN, LOUIS. Criticism in the Making. 1929. [Chapter I, "The Aim and Method of Higher Literary Studies."]

PICCOLI, RAFFAELLO. Italian Humanities: An Inaugural Lecture [University of Cambridge]. 1929.

SHERMAN, STUART P. Critical Woodcuts. 1926.

———. The Main Stream. 1927.

ZEITLIN, JACOB, AND HOMER WOODBRIDGE. Life and Letters of Stuart P. Sherman. 2 vols. 1929. [Especially Volume II, chapters XXIX-XXXIV.]

ELLIOTT, G. R. "Stuart Sherman and the War Age." *The Bookman*, April-May, 1930.

CANBY, HENRY SEIDEL, William Rose Benét, and Amy Loveman. Saturday Papers. 1921. [Essays from the Literary Review of the New York Evening Post.]

———. Definitions: Essays in Contemporary Criticism. 1922. Definitions, Second Series. 1924.

CANBY, HENRY SEIDEL. American Estimates. 1929.
VAN DOREN, CARL. Contemporary American Novelists, 1900–1920. 1923.
———. The Roving Critic. 1923.
———. Many Minds. 1924.

HISTORY—PROPHECY

BOURNE, RANDOLPH. Youth and Life. 1913.
———. History of a Literary Radical and Other Essays. Edited with an Introduction by Van Wyck Brooks. 1920.
EASTMAN, MAX. Enjoyment of Poetry. 1913. [Based on a contrast between the practical and the poetic points of view.]
MACY, JOHN. The Spirit of American Literature. 1913.
BROOKS, VAN WYCK. America's Coming-of-Age. 1915.
———. Letters and Leadership. 1918.
———. The Ordeal of Mark Twain. 1920.
———. The Pilgrimage of Henry James. 1925.
MUMFORD, LEWIS. The Story of Utopias. 1922.
———. Sticks and Stones. 1924.
———. The Golden Day. 1926.
———. Herman Melville. 1929.
WHIPPLE, T. K. Spokesmen: Modern Writers and American Life. 1928. ["To two writers . . . my indebtedness is such as to require particular mention"—Max Eastman and Van Wyck Brooks.]
STEARNS, HAROLD E. (ed.). Civilization in the United States: An Inquiry by Thirty Americans. 1922. ["The nucleus of this group was brought together" by the common interests of Van Wyck Brooks and the editor.]
———. America and the Young Intellectual. 1921.
MIMS, EDWIN. Adventurous America. 1929. ["The story of Randolph Bourne and his flaming zeal, and the more intellectual criticism of Van Wyck Brooks and his colleagues awoke answering echoes." Lewis Mumford's concluding words in The Golden Day "are the summons to the militant and adventurous souls of today."]

READINGS

HUMANISM IN THE TWENTIETH CENTURY

BABBITT, IRVING. Literature and the American College. 1908.
———. The New Laokoon. 1910.
———. The Masters of Modern French Criticism. 1912.
———. Rousseau and Romanticism. 1919.
———. Democracy and Leadership. 1924.
MORE, PAUL ELMER. Shelburne Essays. Eleven series, 1904–21. [Especially the sixth, seventh, and eighth series.]
———. The Greek Tradition. 5 vols. 1917–27.
———. The Demon of the Absolute (New Shelburne Essays, Vol. I). 1929.
———. "A Revival of Humanism." *The Bookman*, March, 1930.
BROWNELL, W. C. Criticism. 1914.
———. Standards. 1917.
SHERMAN, STUART P. Matthew Arnold: How to Know Him. 1917.
———. On Contemporary Literature. 1917.
MATHER, FRANK JEWETT, JR. A History of Italian Painting. 1923.
———. Modern Painting. 1927.
FRYE, P. H. Romance and Tragedy. 1922.
———. Visions and Chimeras. 1929.
FOERSTER, NORMAN. Nature in American Literature. 1923.
———. American Criticism. 1928.
———. The American Scholar. 1929.
———. (ed.). Humanism and America: Essays on the Outlook of Modern Civilization. 1930 (February). [Essays by Louis T. More, Irving Babbitt, Paul Elmer More, G. R. Elliott, T. S. Eliot, Frank Jewett Mather, Jr., Alan Reynolds Thompson, Robert Shafer, Harry Hayden Clark, Stanley P. Chase, Gorham B. Mumson, Bernard Bandler II, Sherlock Bronson Gass, and Richard Lindley Brown.]
SHAFER, ROBERT. Progress and Science. 1922.
———. Christianity and Naturalism. 1926.
———. "What Is Humanism?" *Virginia Quarterly Review*, April, 1930.

TOWARD STANDARDS

SHAFER, ROBERT. "The Definition of Humanism." *The Hound and Horn,* Summer, 1930.

ELLIOTT, G. R. The Cycle of Modern Poetry. 1929.

———. "Mr. More and the Gentle Reader." *The Bookman,* April, 1929.

COLLINS, SEWARD. "Farewell to the 'Twenties" [Chronicle and Comment]. *The Bookman,* January, 1930.

———. "Where Youth Is Turning" [Chronicle and Comment]. *The Bookman,* March, 1930.

———. "Criticism in America." *The Bookman,* June, July and August, 1930.

MUNSON, GORHAM. The Dilemma of the Liberated. 1930.

M'EACHRAN, F. "Humanism and Tragedy." *The Nineteenth Century and After,* July, 1929.

RICHARDS, PHILIP S. "Irving Babbitt." *The Nineteenth Century and After,* April and May, 1928.

———. "An American Platonist." *The Nineteenth Century and After,* April, 1929. [On Paul Elmer More.]

MERCIER, LOUIS J. A. Le mouvement humaniste aux États-Unis. 1928. [On Brownell, Babbitt, and More in relation to the French humanist tradition.]

GRATTAN, C. HARTLEY (ed.). The Critique of Humanism, A Symposium. 1930 (May). [Essays in opposition to humanism by C. Hartley Grattan, Edmund Wilson, Malcolm Cowley, Henry Hazlitt, Burton Rascoe, Allen Tate, Kenneth Burke, Henry-Russell Hitchcock, Jr., R. P. Blackmur, John Chamberlain, Bernard Bandler II, Yvor Winters, and Lewis Mumford.]

KORFF, H. A. Humanismus und Romantik. 1924. [Five lectures delivered at Frankfurt in 1922. Tracing the idea of humanity from the Renaissance to the time of Goethe, this little work provides a suggestive background for the study of humanism in the 19th and 20th centuries.]

INDEX

Alberti, Leon Baltista, 17, 28.
Alfonso the Magnanimous, 11.
Allen, P. S., footnote, 25.
AMERICAN CARAVAN, THE, footnote, 135.
AMERICA'S COMING-OF-AGE, 110, 114 and footnote, 115, 118.
AMERICAN CRITICISM, footnote, 193; footnote, 199.
AMERICAN HISTORICAL REVIEW, footnote, 125.
AMERICAN SCHOLAR, THE, footnote, 81.
Anderson, Sherwood, 88-89, 137, 194.
Appreciation, as opposed to critical evaluation, 64.
Aristotle, 14, 173, 188, 190, 207.
Arnold, Matthew, 46-47, 48, 71, 72, 73, 109, 117, 131; footnote, 142; footnote, 185; 193; footnote, 202; 209, 210.
ASPECTS OF LITERATURE, footnote, 184; footnote, 189.

Babbitt, Irving, 3, 44, 85, 128; footnote, 157; 199 and footnote, 206, 207, 209.
BACKWARD GLANCE, A, footnote, 143.
Bacon, Francis, 39, 40, 79.
Beauty, Croce's definition, 172; humanism's concern with, 172 ff.
Beebe, William, 3.
Bell, Clive, footnote, 45; 61.
Bembo, 13.
Bierce, Ambrose, 117, 124.
Blake, William, 128.
Boccaccio, 16.
Boeckh, August, 36.
Boileau, 72.
Bopp, Franz, 36.
Bourne, Randolph, 105, 106 ff., 112; footnote, 135; footnote, 138.
Brett, G. S., 79 and footnote.

Brooks, Van Wyck, 105, 106, 108, 110-119, 122, 124-125, 131, 133; footnote, 135; footnote, 138.
Brown, Carleton, 3.
Brownell, W. C., footnote, 157.
Browning, Robert, 164.
Budaeus, 24.
Burckhardt, J., footnote, 5; footnote, 9; 13; footnote, 17; 19; footnote, 21.
Burnet, J., footnote, 172.
Burroughs, John, 108.

CAMBRIDGE HISTORY OF AMERICAN LITERATURE, footnote, 84; footnote, 156; footnote, 157.
Canby, Henry S., 84, 91 ff.; footnote, 138; footnote, 169.
Carlyle, Thomas, 134, 195.
Century Magazine, The, footnote, 84.
Cerf, Barry, footnote, 157.
Cervantes, 33.
Chapman, John Jay, footnote, 157.
Chatterton, Thomas, 115.
Chesterton, G. K., 199-211.
Christian Humanists, 19.
Christianity, its relation to Humanism, 5, 19-20, 198 ff.
Cicero, 13, 26.
CIVILIZATION OF THE ITALIAN RENAISSANCE, footnote, 5; footnote, 9; footnote, 17; footnote, 19; footnote, 21.
CIVILIZATION IN THE UNITED STATES, footnote, 138.
Cohen, Morris R., footnote, 45.
Coleridge, Samuel T., 46, 71, 72; footnote, 167; 168.
Colet, 23; footnote, 30.
Cooper, Lane, 208.
Coster, G., footnote, 170.

[219]

INDEX

INDEX

HISTORY OF A LITERARY RADICAL AND OTHER ESSAYS, 108.
Hobbes, Thomas, 147.
Holmes, Oliver W., 111.
Hound and Horn, The, footnote, 199.
Houston, P. H., footnote, 157.
Howells, W. D., 124, 127, 137.
Humanism, historical use of the term, 4; relation of science to, 4; relation of Christianity to, 5; humanism and Humanism defined, 6, *202;* Renaissance H., 7-8; Italian H. and Transalpine H., 8 ff.; characterizing mark of Greek h., 19; of Erasmus, 27 ff.; the decline of, 34; the need of a new, 40-41; Lewis Mumford and, 127 ff.; in the twentieth century, 136 ff.; of Walt Whitman, 141-143; its emphasis upon the independence of the past and present, 144 ff.; realism and romanticism opposed to, 150; the positive contribution of the naturistic movement to, 152; "the new humanists," 156 and footnote, 157; attack by defenders of naturism, 157; fundamental assumptions of, 157 ff.; doctrine and discipline of, 165 ff.; its relation to religion, 171, 198; the æsthetic of, 172; critical method of, 183 ff.; philosophy of, 188; its relation with the problem of an American literature and culture, 190 ff.
HUMANISM AND AMERICA, footnote, 133.
Hutchinson, A. S. M., 96-97.
Huxley, T. H., 35, 52, 146.

IF WINTER COMES, 96.
Imagination, the human or ethical as distinct from the natural or pathetic, 167.
Impressionism, history of the movement 42 ff.; defined, 47; versus tradition, 69 ff.; its critical method, 195-196.
Intensity, its use in critical terminology, 173.
Italian Humanism, 8 ff.

Jackson, Dr. J. A., footnote, 170.
James, Henry, 109, 124, 137.
James, William, 109, 124.
Jebb, Sir Richard C., 73.
Jeffrey, Lord, 89.
Jerome, Saint, footnote, 30.
Johns Hopkins Alumni Magazine, footnote, 147.
Johnson, Dr., 69, 71, 72, 99, 178.
Journalism, critical, 75 ff.; scholarship and, 82; creed of historical, 86; H. S. Canby and critical, 91 ff.; purpose of literary, 95.
JUST NERVES, footnote, 170.

Kittredge, Professor, 3.

Lamartine, Alphonse, 117.
Lamb, Charles, 46, 62.
Lee, Sidney, 39.
LEGACY OF GREECE, THE, footnote, 172.
Lemaitre, Jules, 44, 55-56.
Lessing, Gotthold Ephraim, 35, 71, 72.
LETTERS AND LEADERSHIP, 110.
Lewis, Sinclair, 89, 137.
Lewisohn, Ludwig, 44.
LIFE AND LETTERS OF STUART P. SHERMAN, footnote, 85; footnote, 88.
Lindsay, Vachel, 137.
Lippmann, Walter, 3.
Literary Review, 91.
Literary weekly, function of the, 91.
Locke, John, 147.
Longfellow, Henry W., 123, 137, 142-143.
Lovett, Robert Morss, footnote, 45. 63.
Lowell, James R., 111, 112, 137, 156; footnote, 167.
Luther, Martin, 28, 29.

Macaulay, Lord, 195.
MacDowell, Edward, 109.
Macy, John, footnote, 138.
Maeterlinck, Maurice, 108, 113.
MAIN STREAM, THE, footnote, 87.
MAIN STREET, 99.
MAKING OF THE MODERN MIND, THE, footnote, 6.
Malatesta, Sigismondo, 21.
MANY MINDS, footnote, 84.

INDEX

Marquis, Don, 88.
Masters, Edgar Lee, 122, 137.
Materialen zur Kunde des Älteren Englischen Dramas, 85.
Mather, F. J., Jr., footnote, 157.
Mazzini, Giuseppe, 134.
Maurras, Monsieur, 3.
Medici, Cosimo de', 11.
Melville, Herman, 117, 124; footnote, 125.
Mencken, H. L., footnote, 45; 47; footnote, 138.
Miller, Dickinson S., footnote, 45.
Milton, John, 22, 33, 145, 174, 178, 193.
Mirandola, Pico della, 22.
MODERN BOOK OF CRITICISM, A, 44.
Modern Language Notes, 85.
Molière, 33.
Monism, the naturistic assumption of, 159, 161-162.
More, Paul Elmer, 3, 44, 85; footnote, 157; 207.
Mornet, 77.
Mumford, Lewis, 105, 119-135; footnote, 138.
Murray, Gilbert, 72, 73, 208.
Murry, J. Middleton, footnote, 45; 69; footnote, 184; footnote, 190.

Nation, The, footnote, 84, 91.
Nationalism, Randolph Bourne's plea for an American, 109; Van Wyck Brooks' interpretation of American n. in letters, 110 ff.; Lewis Mumford's relation to the new, 119-135; the critical revolt and its emphasis upon the need of an American culture, 138 ff.; humanism's relation with the problem of an American n., literary and cultural, 190 ff.
Naturism, the tendency of Renaissance humanism toward, 18, 22; the present age of, 18; a development of humanism, 34 ff.; modern scholarship's relation to, 38; the historical attitude in criticism a result of, 77; Rousseau the first spokesman of, 78; its influence upon current conceptions, 145-146; positive contribution of, 152 ff.; attack upon

humanism by defenders of, 157; deterministic monism of, 158-159; assumptions of, 165; anarchy the product of pure romanticism and, 168; the æsthetic of, 172 ff.; philosophy of, 188; humanism and religion allied in opposition to, 201.
New Adelphi, The, footnote, 199.
NEW AMERICAN CARAVAN, THE, footnote, 133.
New Freeman, The, footnote, 133.
New Republic, The, 45 and footnote, 69, 91; footnote, 128; footnote, 133.
Newton, Isaac, 147.
Nicholas V, 11.
Nietzsche, F., 58, 134.
Nitze, William Albert, 39.
Nolhac, Pierre de, footnote, 33.
Norris, Frank, 137.
Norton, Charles Eliot, 156.

ON LIFE AND LETTERS, footnote, 158.
ON TRANSLATING HOMER, footnote, 185.
ORDEAL OF MARK TWAIN, THE, 110, 114.
Ossian, 35.
OUTWITTING OUR NERVES, footnote, 170.

Paganism, historical use of the term, 4.
Pater, Walter, 47-54, 62.
Pattee, Fred Lewis, footnote, 106.
Percy, Thomas, 35.
Petrarch, 16, 34.
Phelps, William Lyon, 108.
Phidias, 207.
Piccolomini, Aeneas, 9.
PILGRIMAGE OF HENRY JAMES, THE, 110, 114.
Pindar, 207.
Pinean, footnote, 30.
Plato, 145, 156; footnote, 158; 173, 189, 207.
Poe, Edgar Allan, 113, 194, 196.
"Poet-scholar," Burckhardt's term, 4, 13.
POETICAL WORKS, of Lowell, footnote, 167-168.
Poggio, 11, 20.
Poliziano, 12, 13.
Pope, Alexander, 61.
Potter, Dr. Francis, 3.

INDEX

PROSE WORKS, of Lowell, footnote, 167.
PROSE WORKS, of Walt Whitman, footnote, 142.
Protagoras, 68, 69.
PSYCHOANALYSIS FOR NORMAL PEOPLE, footnote, 170.
PSYCHOLOGY, ANCIENT AND MODERN, footnote, 79.
PUBLICATIONS OF THE MODERN LANGUAGE ASSOCIATION, footnote, 78; footnote, 82; 85.

Rabelais, 34.
Racine, 33.
Randall, J. H., footnote, 6.
Realism, of the early twentieth century, 136 ff.; its defeat of and kinship with romanticism, 149-150; contribution of naturism to, 152; limitations of scientific, 153, 160; the idea of the organic in, 173; intention of, 187 ff.
REINTERPRETATION OF AMERICAN LITERATURE, THE, footnote, 118.
Religion, humanism's relation to, 171-172, 198 ff.
RELIQUES, Percy's, 35.
Renaissance Humanism, 7 ff.
Revival of Learning, the movement, 11 ff.
REVIVAL OF LEARNING, THE, footnote, 13; footnote, 21.
Riggs, Dr. A. F., footnote, 169.
Robinson, Edwin Arlington, 136-137.
Romanticism, a phase of the naturistic Renaissance, 34 ff.; relation of impressionism to, 46; its judgment of the fundamental critical virtue, 50; inner unity of scientific movement and, 77-78; influence upon modern criticism, 79 ff.; H. S. Canby on, 99; of Lewis Mumford, 128; the revolt of realism against, 136 ff.; the nineteenth century movement a revival of the Middle Ages and the Renaissance, 144-145; the way prepared by Rousseau for nineteenth century, 148; the movement characterized, 148-149; defeat of, 149; its kinship with naturalism, 149-150; limitations of, 153, 160; objective of, 166; anarchy the product of pure

naturalism and, 168; the idea of the organic in, 173; philosophy of, 188.
Rousseau, Jean Jacques, 35, 50, 78, 147-148, 151.
Ruskin, John, 134.

SACRED WOOD, THE, footnote, 182.
Sainte-Beuve, Charles, 46, 49, 77, 79, 80, 102, 117.
Salisbury, Helen M., footnote, 170.
Samson, Leon, 3.
Sandburg, Carl, 137.
Sandys, J. E., footnote, 9; 19, 21; footnote, 36.
Sarton, George, footnote, 5.
Saturday Review of Literature, 91.
Schiller of Oxford, 3.
Schiller, Johann Christoph Friedrich, 35.
Schlegel, August Wilhelm von, 35; footnote, 59; footnote, 167.
Schlegel, Friedrich, 35.
Scholarship, modern literary, 37 ff.; criticism and, 81; journalism and, 82; creed of historical, 86.
Science, its relation to humanism, 4-5; the movement a phase of the naturistic Renaissance, 34 ff.; inner unity of romanticism and, 77-78; in relation to modern criticism, 79 ff.; (in literature) point of view contrasted with that of humanism, 129; contrasted with romanticism, 149; contribution of naturism to, 152; the beginning of humanism in, 172.
SECOND AMERICAN CARAVAN, THE, footnote, 135.
Shafer, Robert, footnote, 157.
Shaftesbury, Earl of, 147, 150.
Shakespeare, 33, 35, 145, 177-179.
Shelley, Percy Bysshe, 148.
Sherman Stuart P., 84 ff.; footnote, 157; 210.
Smith, Logan Pearsall, footnote, 181.
Smith, Preserved, 28, 31.
Socrates, 30, 68, 129.
Sophocles, 177, 179, 207, 208.
Spingarn, J. E., footnote, 14; 58; footnote, 59.
SPIRIT OF AMERICAN LITERATURE, THE, 137.

[223]

INDEX

How are historical criticism
related to impressionistic?

How is Pater's Intro. paradoxical
in the light of his Conclusion

How did romantic criticism contain
the germ of impressionism? Of expressionism?

The relation of journalism to historical scholarship
Of both to romanticism?